27

Selected Poems of
August Strindberg

Selected Poems of
August Strindberg

Edited and Translated by
Lotta M. Löfgren

Southern Illinois University Press
Carbondale and Edwardsville

Library of Congress Cataloging-in-Publication Data

Strindberg, August, 1849–1912.
    [Poems. Selections]
    Selected poems of August Strindberg / edited and
    translated by Lotta M. Löfgren.
        p. ; cm.
    I. Löfgren, Lotta M., 1951– II. Title.
PT9809.A25 L64 2002
839.71'6—dc21
ISBN 0-8093-2463-6 (cloth : alk. paper)   2002018813

Printed on recycled paper. ♻

The paper used in this publication meets the mini-
mum requirements of American National Standard
for Information Sciences—Permanence of Paper for
Printed Library Materials, ANSI Z39.48-1992. ∞

for Elizabeth and Lars

Contents

from
Poems in Verse and Prose

Contents

Acknowledgments

I OWE SEVERAL of my colleagues at the University of Virginia a large debt for their support in this endeavor. Cecil Lang, Arthur Kirsch, and Margareta Mattsson offered their wisdom and advice when I embarked on this project; Gordon Braden stepped in at a crucial moment. Others offered their tireless encouragement when I most needed it, especially Martin Battestin and George Garrett, whose selfless generosity has influenced generations of scholars and writers.

I wish to express my appreciation to the American-Scandinavian Foundation for awarding this work the 2000 American-Scandinavian Translation Prize and for offering much needed support to translators who labor in the shadows of scholarship, unsung and indispensable. In conjunction with the award, my translations of "Saturday Evening" and "Street Pictures" appeared in the autumn 2000 issue of *Scandinavian Review.* My introduction to Professor George Schoolfield of Yale University is a significant additional reward; I am deeply indebted to him for his help in piloting my humble craft to a safe harbor. I thank the editors of Southern Illinois University Press, especially Karl Kageff, for all their help.

My thanks to my friend Lynn Hamilton for her gentle push that put me back on track. Throughout the years, my parents, Lars and Ingeborg Löfgren, have shared their knowledge of Swedish culture, literature, and language; this work would have looked very different if not for their advice. Finally, I wish to thank my children, Elizabeth and Lars Casteen, for simply being: they have given me life, hope, and perseverance. To them, I dedicate this translation.

Selected Poems of
August Strindberg

Introduction

AUGUST STRINDBERG (1849–1912) published three volumes of verse, *Dikter på vers och prosa* (Poems in Verse and Prose) in 1883, *Sömngångarnätter på vakna dagar* (Sleepwalking Nights on Awake Days) in 1884 ("Uppvaknandet" ["The Awakening"] was added to the 1890 edition), and *Ordalek och småkonst* (Word Play and Minor Art), first published in 1902, reissued with an expanded text in 1905. Because it spans a large portion of his career, Strindberg's verse illustrates his growth as an artist from an angle new to English-speaking readers. To date, only isolated poems have been translated into English, mostly in Swedish-language textbooks; the only exception is a 1978 translation of *Sleepwalking Nights* by Arvid Paulson.[1] *Poems* is of considerable historical interest, although individual poems are sometimes forgettable: Strindberg is a pioneering realist who introduced a new kind of satirical verse and free verse into the Swedish canon. The poems of *Sleepwalking Nights* contain moments of powerful lyricism but are most known for their polemical thrust; they trace Strindberg's debates with the world—and with himself—as he moved toward Inferno, his psychic crisis of the mid-1890s. *Word Play and Minor Art* contains highly experimental, varied, and often brilliant verse, at times akin to surreal poetry but antedating it by more than twenty years; the volume is a remarkable artistic achievement. I have selected for this volume poems that illustrate Strindberg's strengths, his versatility, and his development as a poet. It is my hope that readers who know Strindberg mostly from his plays, which have long been available in English, will here find a Strindberg in many ways familiar, in his ideas and beliefs (and perhaps also in his ability to aggravate and fascinate simultaneously), but also fresh, a Strindberg capable of humor, of true delicacy, and of significant lyrical force. Above all, I hope that readers will see that verse and drama are often intimately connected in Strindberg's best works: the drama frequently achieves richness through its verse; the poetry is best when it is most dramatic. As he matures as a poet, Strindberg discovers that drama in verse can reside not only in description, story telling, and dialogue but also in the meter, in the song itself.

In the autobiographical novel *The Son of a Servant,* August Strindberg insists that poetry interested him little in his youth. Strindberg bluntly describes his alter ego Johan's feelings for poetry: "Johan couldn't stand poetry. It was fake, untrue, he thought. People didn't talk in that way and seldom thought such beautiful things" (SS 18, 175–76; SV 20, 134).[2] Strindberg's suspiciousness of poetry was intensified by his exposure to the Signature poets in Uppsala, a group of poets formed by the Norwegian Lorentz Dietrichson in 1860. The poets who gathered under his wing wrote an idyllic, facile, romantic poetry that became the poetic standard of the time. In "Om det allmänna missnöjet, dess orsaker och botemedel" ("On Universal Discontentment, Its Causes and Cures"), Strindberg, discussing his conception of poetry in the early 1880s, clearly has the Signatures in mind:

> The poet is a person who writes verse, more or less good. He is sup-posed to talk in images, and usually the whole value of the poem con-sists in an image, that is in saying one thing and meaning another. Poems are not allowed to treat any of life's more important questions, for a poem is supposed to amuse, arouse pleasant feelings; pretend that there are no ugly sides to life; misery, darkness, accidents, crimes; should preferably say polite things to people, preferably to those in power. (SS 16, 49)

Because Strindberg cared little for poetry as a young man, poetical influences on his own verse are slight. As Strindberg relates in *The Son of a Servant,* he was during his childhood exposed only to those poets whose works he found on his conservative middle-class father's bookshelves, poets who, though con-siderably better than the Signatures, still failed to move him.[3] The German poet Heinrich Heine was a notable exception: his verse strongly flavors the free verse in *Poems,* such as "Sunset on the Sea" and "Indian Summer." As Olof Lagercrantz notes, Strindberg imitated Heine's "coquettish reference to himself" and his polemics: "their position was similar; both fought an official, academic, and dishonest homeland and its more or less official representatives."4

One might ask why Strindberg chose to write poetry in the 1880s, since he, at that time, openly scorned verse. The answer: he wanted approval from those he mocked. "He, who despised the whole game," he writes in *The Son of a Servant,* "would not have striven for such a dubious honor as being able to write poetry, but as long as 'the others' valued that sport so highly, he had to show them that he could do it too, if he felt like it" (SS 19, 196; SV 21, 153). "The others" refers to the literary establishment, especially the Signature poets. Strindberg's decision to write *Poems in Verse and Prose* had less to do with his interest in poetry as an art form and more to do with his political agenda. He even openly condemns the art in his curious foreword to *Poems.* He flippantly anticipates criticism by averring that he is perfectly aware of the metrical irregularities of his poems but that he does not care, "since I consider verse to shackle thought in unnecessary bonds, which a newer age will discard," and "since I consider my thought more important than a metrical foot or a rhyme" (SS 13, 7; SV 15, 9). Two ruling principles of *Poems,* then, are Strindberg's desire, on one hand, to prove to the Signature poets that he could write poetry as well as they, and, on another, to ridicule them and defy their poetic principles by openly mocking them in his poetry and by including in his own poems a barrage of forbidden elements: slang, satire, ugly (and sometimes scatological) metaphors, uneven meter, free verse, prose, bad smells, dirt, ragged people.

Strindberg's early ambivalence about poetry is the result of more complex forces at war in him than the combined dislike and envy of the Signature poets, an ambivalence one needs to understand in order to more fully comprehend the poetry. He was taught a strict Pietism by his mother, a devotion presumably strengthened by her death when he was thirteen. Coupled with his father's admonitions of duty and usefulness, these forces made him feel guilty about pursuing his writing because it was such a pleasurable activity and essentially useless. The combined influences of his mother and father told him that authorship was sinful; as a result, he tried to make his writing as "useful" and "ugly" as possible to ease his own conscience. Strindberg's suspiciousness of art juxtaposed with his great love of his vocation created an almost intolerable dilemma for him. It would be difficult to overemphasize the importance of this conflict to Strindberg's career. It ruled his life and his work until after the Inferno crisis in the mid-1890s. It caused him to create polemical writings that are often petulant and tedious; many poems in *Poems in Verse and Prose* and *Sleepwalking Nights on Awake Days* are colored by his need to be useful and socially relevant. In a tormented letter to the Norwegian writer Björnstjerne Björnson dated 1884, Strindberg himself expounds on his inner conflict:

> Here is the dilemma! In order to be useful I have to be read! In order to be read I have to write "art" but I consider "art" immoral. Therefore: either die, with a clean soul, or continue with a for me immoral activity!
>
> Answer that question! Then, when I have pondered and struggled, comes that black devil who sits in my heart, and sneers at the whole thing, and then the epicurean art spirit in me awakens and I yearn for the pleasure that creating art gives me, and it is a colossal pleasure, but herein lies the immorality. [. . .] Oh this damned aesthetics! The beautiful, yes it lives, and I too worship the beautiful, but NATURE! You cannot see nature because your eyes are destroyed by works of Art, arrogant people's miserable deceptions! (*Letters* 4, 144–45)

By Strindberg's own account, other forces were at war within. Indeed, one could argue that Strindberg was on all levels an ambivalent and divided human being and that this quality in him was responsible for the best and worst in his writings. It occasioned his misogyny and paranoia but also his vibrancy, unpredictability, and innovativeness. He considered himself a contradictory mixture of his mother's softness and his father's hardness, as he relates in *The Son of a Servant*:

> Ambitious and weak-willed; unscrupulous when he had to be, and obsequious when he didn't; great self-confidence mingled with profound dejection; sensible and impractical; hard and weak. This dualism in his character was a natural consequence of his double upbringing in Christianity and positivism. As a transitional being he contained new and old deposits of idealism and realism. With his two points of view, the little one of the present and the great one of the future, he had constantly to see things from at least two sides. Unfortunately, his volatile temperament did not always allow him to decide which viewpoint to adopt. (SS 19, 32–33; SV 21, 27–28)

He struggled all his life with the idealist and realist within, seeking truth simultaneously in the tangible and the transcendent; he is by turns a skeptic and a seeker. He is also by turns compliant and rebellious. His literary works offer many illustrations of his desire to be led and his subsequent anger at any suspected attempts to control him. He consistently believed that all women, many men, and, above all, God tried to usurp his strength and leave him powerless; this belief caused him in the 1880s to develop a theory of "the battle of brains" ("hjärnornas kamp") reminiscent of, if not inspired by, Nietzsche's ideas of the Superman. In the same vein, although he at times expressed great admiration for other writers, he also feared that their influence would sap his own creative strength; consequently, throughout his life, he openly condemned authors he had previously praised, Björnstjerne Björnson and Henrik Ibsen, among others. This paranoia of influence drove him to break new ground at nearly every step and to create enemies, which fueled his need to feel misunderstood, set apart. His works are from beginning to end replete with maligned soothsayers, who, especially in his later works, appear as "the wanderer," the loner who, unappreciated and mistreated, nevertheless serves society. He had a highly romantic notion of his mission to spread the gospel of realism and other social and literary reforms; his maligned heroes, always thinly camouflaged autobiographical characters, tend to vacillate between self-pity and satire in their response to the world. Strindberg is by turns a conventional man, comfortable in his middle-class surroundings, and the social rebel and iconoclast, compelled to destroy the old and break new ground. As a result, his works by turns celebrate order, whether social or cosmic, and seek to overthrow that order. The warring urges to destroy and preserve order touch all aspects of his writing, his poems not the least, including their philosophy, their language, and even their meter.

Strindberg found support for his personal inclinations in the works of a number of philosophers. Because of his need to write useful—that is polemical—verse and because of his relative lack of interest in poetry early in his literary career, these philosophers flavor his poetry more than do other poets. The Danish philosopher Georg Brandes' writings filled him with "that suspiciousness of abstract idealism that accompanies him throughout the 1880's."[5] Strindberg saw Brandes as the most important proponent in the new movement to return the ethical to art and remove the tyranny of the aesthetic. Brandes introduced him to Shakespeare; this happy event helped him to emerge a few years later as Sweden's pioneering realist with the prose (and first) version of the play *Master Olof* (1872). The same year, Strindberg was introduced to Kierkegaard through *Either-Or,* which he read "with fear and trembling" (SS 18, 386; SV 20, 295). The existentialist Kierkegaard rejected Hegel's belief in the ultimate possibility of the synthesis of dialectical forces. Ironically, Hegel's belief in synthesis and his optimistic reliance on reason as a path to divinity well articulate Strindberg's own professed desire for a resolution to his own dualistic struggles. That Strindberg could not accept Hegel but instead championed the philosophers who opposed him points both to the restlessness of Strindberg's soul and to the fact that his need to sustain the fissure in his own psyche was at least as strong as his desire to heal it. Kierkegaard's work fueled Strindberg's anti-aesthetic impulses, which bridged in Strindberg's mind the teachings of Brandes and Kierkegaard, despite their profound differences. The above-cited letter to Björnson suggests that Strindberg was a follower of Rousseau. He encountered Rousseau's treatises in the early 1870s; he would, with a few lapses, remain a Rousseauian all his life. Rousseau's contempt for culture and romantic appraisal of nature found in Strindberg a willing disciple. At this time, Strindberg discovered the writings of Arthur Schopenhauer, who became an even more important figure for him. Schopenhauer's interest in Eastern philosophy influenced Strindberg's own flirtations with the occult. Schopenhauer's reliance on the intellect to explain existence and his simultaneous formulation of the will as part of the universal and inexplicable soothed Strindberg's own bifurcated nature. Early and late, Schopenhauer's extreme, ideal pessimism, focusing as it does on human misery and the desirability of nonexistence, offered Strindberg a blend of skepticism and mysticism he inevitably found attractive. In 1872, Strindberg read Thomas Henry Buckle's *History of Civilization in England,* which he used as yet another weapon against the Pietist still resident within. It is a mark of the keenness of Strindberg's internal struggle that he can be simultaneously fascinated by Buckle and Kierkegaard. But, for all their differences, they shared the belief that ultimate truth is unattainable, if not nonexistent. And Buckle's positivist insistence on looking at human life, even man's spiritual side, as a part of physical nature served as a corollary to the theories of Schopenhauer and Rousseau. The attractiveness to Strindberg of these particular philosophers suggests how torn he was between embracing idealism and championing rationalism. They helped support Strindberg's attitude toward his poetry and toward his quest for truth, in this world and beyond, especially in *Sleepwalking Nights*.

In spite of Strindberg's frequent pronouncements against poetry in his early career, he himself made several forays into verse before the publication of *Poems* in 1883. He wrote two early verse plays, *Hermione* (1869) and *I Rom* (In Rome) (1870), both in iambs. The blank verse in *Hermione* flows fairly naturally, although it never rises to great lyrical moments; even in his early verse, Strindberg keeps his verse akin to speech, fluid but rather flat. *In Rome*, written almost exclusively in rhymed iambic pentameter, sounds more stilted and includes a discussion on how to write poetry: a little wine and a few rhymes are all you need to become a poet. These pronouncements are primarily intended as a jab at the Signatures, but arguably Strindberg's precepts for his own poetry in this play are not much more stringent. He probably penned these plays in verse because of their subject matter and because lofty verse-plays were the fashion at the time. In the play *Den fredlöse* (Exiled) (1871), Strindberg already displays his ability to fuse lyricism and drama; the prose play contains verse passages to illustrate the characters' more personal and passionate moments. The most significant example of verse from Strindberg's pen before the publication of *Poems* is the verse version of the play *Master Olof*. It blends prose and Strindberg's first experimentations with the *knittel* verse form that he would perfect in *Sleepwalking Nights*. This version grew out of the literary establishment's insistence that a prose play was not a viable art form; Strindberg consequently had to rework the early prose version of the play, adding verse passages, in order to get it accepted by a Stockholm theater. One can understand Strindberg's subsequent suspicions of the literary establishment; it was entirely blind to the brilliance of the first version of the play. Although the prose version of *Master Olof* is now generally considered superior to the verse version, the latter has in places achieved compaction, even dramatic enhancement, through the use of verse. With *Lucky Per's Journey,* written in 1882, Strindberg settled upon a pattern he was to repeat throughout his career: the play is in prose interspersed with simple songs, akin to folk songs, that lend a folkloric, timeless quality to the works.

Poems in Verse and Prose

Strindberg achieved his first literary success with the publication of the satirical roman-à-clef *The Red Room: Stories from the Lives of Artists and Authors* in 1879, which made him an instant sensation. But in 1882, he published a two-volume revisionist history of Sweden called *Svenska folket* (The Swedish People), containing irreverent revaluations of many Swedish cultural heroes. The public and critics responded bitterly. Strindberg was surprised and deeply hurt by the criticism. In defiance of the critics, in the same year, he penned *Det nya riket: Skildringar från attentatens och jubelfesternas tidevarv* (The New Kingdom: Stories from the Age of Assassination Attempts and Jubilees), an even sharper social satire that far more transparently mocks Sweden's cultural and political elite. An uproar followed, predictably enough. The hypersensitive Strindberg—sensitive to insults directed at *him,* at least—departed Sweden with his family in September 1883, to escape the wrath of his critics and to join the already significant number of Scandinavian expatriate artists on the continent. As a final salvo in the battle against his critics, he spent the summer before his departure at work on *Poems in Verse and Prose,* replete with satirical poems directed at his enemies.

Because of Strindberg's relative isolation from the poetic tradition and the unbridled energy with which he produced his poems, he was an important innovator in *Poems* even when he was a weak poet. Even the bad poems exude a vigor, an immediacy, a tangibility, that revolutionized Swedish poetry. In *A History of Swedish Literature,* Alrik Gustafson suggests that Strindberg's "handling of language is one of the chief miracles of Swedish literature. No Swedish author has the stylistic variety and range, the spontaneity, directness, and economy of phrasing that Strindberg commands. He shook Swedish prose completely loose from its earlier ceremonious, rhetorical propensities, bringing to it a pulsing aliveness and driving intensity that have provided the point of departure for all modern developments in Swedish prose style."[6] The same must be said of his poetry. Strindberg's early verse is revolutionary, in part, because he drew much of his inspiration from prose. He spoke with great admiration of Olaus Petri's[7] historical chronicles (SS 7, 479–86), lauding his courage for writing in Swedish instead of Latin and in a clear, direct style. He admired the eighteenth-century Swedish naturalist Carl von Linné (Linnaeus) for similar reasons. Both influenced his prose style and ultimately also his poetic language, which also strives for directness and honesty.

Poems is divided into four sections. "Youth and Ideals,"[8] containing the earlist poems, offers the reader a glimpse of Strindberg before he became embroiled in the controversy with his critics. It shows him at times imitative of the Signature poets, but at other times remarkably fresh. The most interesting poem in this section is "In Nyström's Studio," in which we find the energy, the visual brilliance, the terse, modern language, the revolutionary realistic and satirical elements that are part of Strindberg's genius. "In Nyström's Studio" condemns Signature poetry much more effectively than the diatribes against it that appear in other poems by simply being so different. Like all Strindberg's best poems, it is intensely dramatic. The two men in the poem are in constant motion, and all the props crowding into the poem have an energy of their own. The language follows suit. Strindberg writes in a racy vernacular, showing off his enormous vocabulary, rejecting the flaccid language of the Signatures, infusing the poem with a lighthearted satire. The poem is replete with mud, sweat, and trash; the sculptor whines, sings, dances, drinks beer—hardly a dignified romantic figure. Typically, the poem is filled with movement, always a Strindbergian strong suit. Here is Strindberg before his goal in writing poetry became revenge on his critics.

"Storms," the section preceding "Youth and Ideals" in *Poems,* contains poems mostly from the 1870s, written about ten years before *Poems* appeared. In contrast to the poems in "Youth and Ideals," many had been published previously. "Sunset on the Sea" is one of the earliest examples of free verse in Swedish. It was written in 1874, only two years after Rimbaud's earliest poems of free verse in French. "Sunset on the Sea" and "Indian Summer" are, as I have mentioned, strongly influenced by the German poet Heinrich Heine. Strindberg's use of metaphor here is new in Swedish poetry. In a jibe at the contentless poetry of the Signatures, he readily confesses in "Sunset on the Sea" to be thinking about nothing. And *his* metaphors about sea and sunset have to do with chemical compounds and half-lit cigars. So self-conscious is Strindberg about using traditional romantic metaphors, about sounding trite and sentimental like the Signatures, that his metaphors have to shock, not just describe and enhance. Yet they do describe and enhance, and in a fresh way. It is a revolutionary poem, highly significant to the development of Swedish poetry.

The first part of "Exile" is one of the strongest in the section. It was probably begun after Strindberg's return from a journey to Norway and France in the autumn of 1876, but he almost certainly wrote some sections later and added to and reworked the poem over a period of several years.[9] In a forceful challenge to the Signature poets, Strindberg rejects the pastoral scene in favor of the city mire. And instead of a mawkish sighing over pretty sunsets, he presents a hung-over main character who may see things in a mist, but a mist created by bar room smoke and eyes made bleary by too much drink. When later the bachelor dreams of childhood days, we see a sentimentality the Signatures may have felt more kinship with, but these memories of childhood consist of concrete, mundane images they would never have noticed: "dressers with protruding bellies," an uncle tapping feet to the music, a grandmother peering at her world through spectacles. The poem well illustrates how closely sentimentality and satire dwell in Strindberg's temperament. The foremost Swedish literary rebel celebrated middle-class life like no other Swedish poet.

The poem's structure, like many of Strindberg's longer poems, is dramatic. Strindberg quickly sketches the scene in a kind of poetic stage direction before introducing the characters. Here he displays the swiftness and certainty that in his prose works made him such a sensation. Verbs sparkle: "dozing," "careering," "clamor," "drizzling," "kneads" paint, in the first stanza, a picture of the small and large in the Stockholm scene while grappling for space on the crowded line. All this is accomplished in a controlled, untortured trochaic pentameter. Lines of pentameter are interspersed with lines of tetrameter and an occasional line of hexameter, but these variations do not awkwardly interrupt the rhythm, as is often the case elsewhere when Strindberg grows impatient or sloppy. By retaining the steady trochaic foot even when the line length varies, he creates a suitable ironic backdrop to the feverish visions described in the poem. In this poem, as in others, after starting out with one metric scheme, Strindberg eventually settles into a comfortable tetrameter as the poem picks up speed. It is one of his favorite meters, to which he returns regularly.

"Wound-Fever" and "High Summer," appearing first and second in the volume, comprise poems written in 1883, just before Strindberg left for France. The poems in "High Summer" are probably written slightly earlier[10] and represent the last moments of calm Strindberg was to feel for several years. The poems of "Wound-Fever" are the ones he calls his "angry [. . .] and beautiful" poems directed at his critics (*Letters 3*, 251). "High Summer" describes his life in the Stockholm archipelago during the summer of 1883. Strindberg passionately loved the archipelago; he wrote of the islands with fondness even when he was most bitter about Swedish people and culture. The two juxtaposed sections remind us of the volatility and variability of Strindberg's temperament.

The poems of "High Summer," filled with love poems to his first wife, Siri, have become some of the most beloved of Strindberg's poems, ironically because they are the "safest." The greatest of these domestic poems is "Summer Evening," since its first appearance the popular favorite of all Strindberg's poems. It infuses the holy stillness of the warm evening with moments of vigor that make it a complex poem in spite of its simple subject matter. Nothing much happens; the only human acts in the course of the poem are the farmhand playing his accordion in the distance and the wife blowing out the final candle. Yet we come across delicate hints of energy: "A flock of woodcocks flies above the trees," in stanza two, and, in the third stanza, the stillness betrays signs of the children's exuberance in the scattered toys. In the final stanza, we learn that storms always threaten beyond the horizon, as is indeed the case, in Strindberg's life and in his art. The alliteration and assonance suffusing the poem anticipate the mature poetry of *Word Play and Minor Art;* they lend the poem a sonorousness that harmonizes perfectly with the stillness of the scene.

"Wound-Fever" contains poem after poem of more or less controlled attacks on Strindberg's critics. The reader must constantly keep in mind that these poems are innovative for their language, imagery, and subject matter, or they are tedious indeed. Many poems contain responses to specific individuals and are perhaps the least interesting to the modern reader, since most allusions are obscure. In other poems in "Wound-Fever," Strindberg's anger leads to a great deal of metrical sloppiness. He repeatedly grabs any convenient meter and grinds away at his enemies. Some poems seem so quickly written that the syntax is awkward and the meaning uncertain. In these angry poems, the music of the line is just not important to Strindberg. If a poem has some kind of meter, even an irregular meter, and if it rhymes, then it satisfies his requirements. In Strindberg's defense, these irregularities are a necessary first step in his decision to give up traditional meter and to experiment with methods more suitable to his style. And a few poems in this section rise well above the others in interest and quality.

"Loki's Curses" is one example. Strindberg here curses "our time's Gods," that is, the cultural and political elite, for trying to stifle him and for mocking his work. "Loki's Curses" became a battle song for a group of Swedish writers that called itself "Young Sweden." The poet Gustaf Fröding writes in *Boken om Strindberg* (The Book about Strindberg): "No one who was alive and young when this poem appeared will forget the powerful impression it created. The younger generation recognized in it the long awaited declaration of war against the prevalent stagnation and slavish obedience to every kind of usurping authority."[11] The allegory of the Norse god Loki in a heroic battle against enemy gods lends a nobility and a grandeur to the poem that many of the other poems lack. Loki is one of Strindberg's many maligned heroes. Strindberg's ironic manipulation of the myth—like the original, Strindberg's Loki is an instigator of chaos; unlike the original, he's a good and necessary, not an evil, force—suggests the influence of Schopenhauer. Loki, the god of fire, shapeless and unpredictable, is in Strindberg's eyes a savior *because* he is a destroyer. As always, Strindberg's word-hoard is vibrant, even fierce, attaining here a holy anger. The meter of "Loki's Curses" is a key element. The trochaic tetrameter is better suited to the Swedish language than the iambic trimeter he uses in other poems of the section, and the stressed first syllable in each line slows the pace somewhat to avoid the silliness of the trimeter. "Loki's Curses" contains few filler words and a more natural diction than many other poems in this section. The language of "Loki's Curses" is both direct and noble, rarely compromising itself to accommodate the meter. Strindberg, as so often happens when he becomes passionate, perhaps goes on too long and diminishes the poem's force, but the passion rings true and powerful throughout.

"The Boulevard System" and "The Epicure" also depart from the peevishness of many other poems in the section. Like "Loki's Curses," "The Boulevard System" was a favorite with Sweden's young intelligentsia eager for destruction of the old order. The Young Sweden members, who fancied themselves nihilists, used the poem as a battle cry.[12] In "The Epicure," Strindberg momentarily gives up anger in favor of humor, with happy results. The poem's central argument is as usual that the coachman (the critic) does not know good wine (Strindberg's art) when he tastes it but prefers porter mixed with strychnine (the poor and often vicious writing of the Signatures and the critics). Yet this poem is a dramatic gem. Here the dramatist creates character with a few swift strokes. The coachman is real, tangible, nonheroic, more than a caricature. And he speaks: his few words, effortlessly dropped into the poem, tell us in an instant who he is. The iambic pentameter—with the usual admixture of tetrameter and hexameter—moves smoothly and well suits the racy language of the poem.

"For the Freedom of Thought" is the section's most innovative and ambitious poem. It condemns the cynical manipulation by government officials of public sentiment, despite the purported intention of celebrating the "freedom of thought" and Gustav II Adolf (Gustavus Adolphus), who in the Thirty Years War kept the world safe for Protestantism. The poem reveals Strindberg's ambivalence toward the aristocracy. He contemns the trappings of polite society and its stupid, nearly bestial rituals at the supper table. But undercurrents of envy flow as well. The maligned hero, who lives on society's periphery and whom we meet here sneering at the revelers in the tavern "King Karl," is not entirely happy about not being invited to the party. Strindberg splendidly illustrates the commotion among the upper crust at the feast, eager to notice and be noticed. The understated satirical thrust is one of his greatest talents. In section two, we see in the jumble "ladies of every kind" and others who "commit" a feast for the freedom of thought. The Archbishop's "beautiful speech" and the singers' "beautiful hymn" tell us volumes about the shallowness of their sentiment. These passages show a clear influence of Dickens, whose works Strindberg read in translation: Dickens, too, relished caricatures of feasting crowds. The poem is an early experiment with the *knittel* verse form Strindberg discovered in the Edda and Swedish folk songs and perfected in *Sleepwalking Nights on Awake Days:* as in Anglo-Saxon poetry, only stressed syllables are counted.[13] Immediately we sense what dramatic and poetic freedom the verse form offers. Strindberg finds in the *knittel* verse a compromise between prose and metric verse that allows him to include those elements that have already made him a sensation as a prose writer. Much of the verse creates stumbling blocks for the reader, but these are variations with a purpose: sections in long, irregular verse accompany the bustling, raucous mob enjoying the feast; these are juxtaposed with more regular, simple verses describing the private contemplations of the reporter and the priest in the third and fourth sections respectively, and, at last, of the author himself in section seven. "For the Freedom of Thought" represents the culmination of his work in *Poems.* Despite a myriad of metrical pratfalls, Strindberg takes the reader on a fascinating journey of discovery: we see in this volume of verse the process of poetic maturation as he realizes that meter can strengthen the poem's message, not just accompany it.

Sleepwalking Nights on Awake Days

August Strindberg wrote *Sleepwalking Nights on Awake Days* after taking up residence in the artist's colony at Grez, a village outside Paris, in 1883. The last poem in *Poems in Verse and Prose,* originally called "Farewell," Strindberg renamed "Sleepwalking Nights (A Fragment): The First Night." Settled in Grez, he completed the first four *Nights* with an urgency rare even for him. He sent off the "First Night" to his publisher on October 19, 1883; by December 23, "The Fourth Night" was finished (SV 15, 372). He wrote to Albert Bonnier, his publisher, "now I am writing my Nights—and I can't stop myself" (*Letters* 3, 357). "The Awakening", in earlier editions "The Fifth Night" (SV 15, 407), Strindberg wrote in 1889, some time after his return to Stockholm in April of that year, more than five years after finishing "The Fourth Night"—hence its stylistic divergence from the other "Nights."

Sleepwalking Nights on Awake Days must be some of the most polemical poems ever written; Björnstjerne Björnson called them "lectures in verse."[14] As I have explained, the polemics were a way for Strindberg to resolve his ambivalence about poetry. When first envisioning *Sleepwalking Nights,* he described the poems, in a letter to Albert Bonnier, as "romantic-satirical-realistic-idealistic" (*Letters* 3, 329), and in a letter to Björnstjerne Björnson, he called them "a struggle with myself" (*Letters* 4, 46). The structure of each of the first four "Nights" is similar: from the present in France the spirit travels at night to Sweden and the past in order to examine various facets of Swedish culture; it then returns to France and the present as dawn approaches. As Henry Olsson explains in his essay on *Sleepwalking Nights,* the French frame was an afterthought on Strindberg's part, added when the work was more than half finished,[15] a way to negatively compare Sweden with France. But that structure breaks down. Strindberg grows increasingly irritated with Paris and homesick for Sweden in the process of writing the poem, even as he condemns Sweden's culture. This adds a curious immediacy to the work: the reader actually participates in Strindberg's growing disillusionment and confusion about where his allegiances lie. *Sleepwalking Nights on Awake Days* stands as a testament to that tension within Strindberg that creates a conflict or dialectic in many of his writings; because his inner conflict actually becomes the central subject-matter of the poem, *Sleepwalking Nights* offers us a unique opportunity for a more complete understanding not only of Strindberg himself but also of his art.

The first four "Nights" systematically discredit Swedish culture. "The First Night" exposes the hypocrisy of the Swedish Lutheran Evangelical state church, her cruelty toward her flock, and her irrelevance to daily life. "The Second Night" challenges the falseness and arrogance of art in its attempt to improve on nature; the poem condemns art's cult of beauty, its uselessness, and finally its elitism. In "The Third Night," Strindberg dismisses the university disciplines of theology, philosophy, history, and law. He argues that they are flawed because they do not make our lives better or teach us anything about the meaning of life, about ultimate truths. "The Fourth Night" attacks natural science for its destruction of nature and for its refusal to tackle humanity's pressing needs; it condemns scientists for wasting their time with arrogant and useless research.

"The Third Night," the strongest poem of the first four "Nights," opens with Strindberg walking in the streets of Paris. He sings with lyrical passion about the ugly in the opening lines, combining powerful poetic images and social criticism, lyricism and realism. He creates what we might call an ironic lyricism or lyrical realism new to the Swedish poetic tradition. It anticipates the poetry of his own *Word Play and Minor Art* and the poetry of later generations. The sounds and meter perfectly reinforce the confusion of his experience in the labyrinthine streets of Paris, without any sacrifice of metrical discipline. Strindberg uses a sustained trochaic tetrameter, softened by at least one dactyl in each line. He perfects in *Sleepwalking Nights* the *knittel* verse he had experimented with in *Master Olof* and "For the Freedom of Thought." He achieves a compelling combination of discipline and versatility in this meter that well accompanies the ironic tension between the lyricism and realism in the content. And as always in Strindberg's best poetry, the poem crackles with action, movement, and energy. Crowds push, vehicles clatter, children cry, dogs bark, people shout; the whole city roars.

The poem gains greater depth through Strindberg's self-irony. In the din, he finds himself seeking the romantic moment he has worked so hard to avoid, for reality is actually becoming too much for him. To escape the commotion of the Paris streets, he flees to a church:

> Not to pray he enters that church,
> Nor to adulate fetishes,
> Merely to relish holy silence,
> Loosen merely the heavy chain,
> Leave behind him sorrow and woe.

Yet the realism immediately undergoes a new transformation, to the grotesque: he discovers that the church has become a temple to utilitarianism. The noisy machines threaten him; they resemble evil beings. Despite Strindberg's suspiciousness of romanticism at this time, his art actually needs a dimension other than realism, just as he needs the dualism in his own character to ensure his survival. The destruction of the romantic therefore leads not to a pristine realism but to a new qualification, or distortion, of reality; for Strindberg, there is no other alternative.

When the spirit resumes his journey in "The Third Night," it flies to the Royal Library in Stockholm, where Strindberg worked before leaving Sweden, to seek truth in learning and knowledge. Predictably, all branches of knowledge disappoint him, for they cannot agree on what truth means, and "when all scream that they have found truth/ Far better then to beat a retreat." Uncertainty about where truth lies and ambivalence about how to find it exists on a prosodic as well as on a polemical level: Strindberg searches for perfection in language as well as for truth. The union of lyricism and realism, however effective it may seem, doesn't satisfy him. So when the scene shifts to the Royal Library in Stockholm and the subject to Strindberg's exposure of learning's hypocrisy, his pilgrimage in quest of a perfect language continues. Moving toward the perfection of language, Strindberg suggests, involves rejecting its distortions. Even the Bible's language proves equivocal; the books squabble with each other until language loses all effectiveness. Despite the poetic control of "The Third Night," Strindberg seems to reject all poetic language, indeed all language, except perhaps that found in newspaper articles, that kind of useful writing that gets at the truth without linguistic embellishment. But he appears to realize, although he does not want to admit it, that language—at least his language—needs embellishment or distortion. Through the process of seeking perfection in his art in "The Third Night," he discovers that the utilitarianism and polemics upon which he has tried to build *Sleepwalking Nights* make for inadequate art. He finds perfection not where he wants to find it, in purely polemical writings, but in the union of realism and lyricism, in the nurturing of the tension and the distortion they create. This tension, in fact, made Strindberg the groundbreaking modernist that he was, a pivotal force in the Swedish literary tradition.

Sleepwalking Nights is indeed Strindberg's "struggle with myself," evincing his need to believe and to doubt simultaneously. This struggle between doubt and faith that cannot—indeed, must not—be resolved creates poetic richness and dramatic complexity. Throughout this "struggle with myself," Strindberg seeks truth. But he can never resolve the dilemma that truth means radically different things to a realist and an idealist, to a doubter and a believer. Strindberg the realist exposes religion, art, and learning as perpetrators of social lies, empty ceremony, abstraction, irrelevancy. But when he searches for the meaning of life, he is an idealist yearning for a higher form of truth in existence, for what ought to be. Strindberg's point of view in *Sleepwalking Nights* is both Socratic and Platonic, skeptical and idealistic. The central dilemma that his need to doubt will not allow him to find answers to his quest for life's meaning and his need to believe will not allow him to end his quest keeps him in a state of turmoil, which fuels his compulsion to write while bringing him close to despair.

In "The Awakening," Strindberg's perception and presentation of reality change dramatically. In the first four "Nights," his task involved stripping reality of all lies and illusions to find its true core and to find what ultimate truth is. As I have suggested, he was never able finally to determine the nature of reality or of truth or to achieve a satisfactory literary realism. In "The Awakening," definitions of real and ideal gradually grow indistinguishable. Strindberg initially seems to find an idyllic union between the real and ideal, as he (the poem is clearly autobiographical) looks out over Stockholm after many years' absence and marvels at its beauty. But as he descends into the city quite another perception replaces the ideal vision. Strindberg experiences not the fluctuation between idealism and skepticism of the previous "Nights" but a passing flirtation with idealism permanently replaced by a reality turned macabre. As in "The Third Night," when the transcendent dimension can no longer counterbalance reality, it becomes absorbed into reality while distorting it. This distortion finds its most extreme expression as Strindberg, walking through the city streets, comes upon the apartment where he and his first wife once lived. In a final attempt, he tries to suffuse reality with a romantic glow: "He attempts to paint for the eye / His former home in rosy-red hues." But he has lost his romantic vision and instead creates an eerie image that nevertheless appears perfectly tangible. Looking into the window, he sees himself sitting there writing, but nothing appears on the paper, and the image looks grotesque: "Dead man's eyes are as large as teacups / Staring darkly with sightless orbs." Even his own imagination persecutes him. Here, Strindberg moves beyond realism and romanticism to surrealism, where feelings not only color reality but actually change it.

The intimations of chaos in "The Third Night" are now manifest. Although Strindberg moves toward a radical new art in "The Awakening," the dissolution of the distinction between real and unreal signals Strindberg's personal dysfunction, a pathological destruction of his essential dualistic vision. Nevertheless, the emotional stress Strindberg experienced in these years, already amounting to severe mental distress and well-advanced paranoia, results in a new elegance and control in "The Awakening." The poem offers perhaps the best example of Strindberg's uncanny ability to translate personal crisis into artistic triumph. The elements of paranoia are perfectly controlled and artistically sound: they develop gradually throughout the poem with startling dramatic effectiveness, from the idealistic scene at the beginning to the nightmarish vision at the end. Yet he cannot long sustain this control. Strindberg does experience an awakening at the poem's close, but it is an awakening into a new nightmare, a limbo where neither reality nor dream offers a foothold, an awakening into hopelessness, not to visions of truth. "The Awakening" was one of the last successful works of art Strindberg was to create for many years. At the time of its completion, Inferno loomed.

After some years on the continent and an unfortunate second marriage, Strindberg sequestered himself in Paris and spent several months in 1896 and 1897 (his Inferno period) isolated, engaged in alchemical and occult experiments. His paranoia seems to have become full-blown: he was persuaded that people were trying to kill him, through electric currents from the adjoining room, for example. He also pronounced himself an atheist during these years, perhaps the single largest cause for his mental dissolution; this was one battle of brains Strindberg lost. In 1897, he started emerging from his Inferno, primarily because he returned to a faith in God. He decided that his psychoses were punishments from God and from what he called "the Powers," a jury that sat in constant judgment on him. Strindberg's need for authority, combined with his paranoid need for order, caused him to formulate a monistic view of a cohesive universe, in his unique adaptation still fraught with misery and chaotic elements. Although his monism owed much to childhood beliefs and personal experience, he discovered kindred spirits in two eighteenth-century Swedish philosophers who helped him formulate his new beliefs: the theosophist Emanuel Swedenborg and the naturalist Carl von Linné. Strindberg writes in *Legends* that "Swedenborg has become my Virgil, who leads me through hell, and I follow him blindly" (SS 28, 294). Swedenborg's theories about correspondences, about a tangible world beyond ours that is actually more real than our own (similar to Schopenhauer's theories of the will), became extremely attractive to Strindberg; *A Dream Play* (1901) well illustrates this new worldview. About Linné's importance, Strindberg expounds in a letter to Torsten Hedlund from Paris in 1896: "I am the naturalist-occultist, like Linné, my great teacher. First physics, then meta——. I want to see with my exterior eyes first and then with the interior" (*Letters* 11, 219). Linné's combination of scientific naturalism and mystical speculation predictably gained Strindberg's enthusiastic approval. Strindberg thus achieved a unique union between the real and the ideal by reinterpreting reality. Or, as Gunnar Brandell puts it in *Strindberg in Inferno*: "Strindberg describes the experiences of a neurotic in a style that aspires to naturalistic exactitude."[16] Linné's theory of Nemesis Divina, which Strindberg interpreted as a cynical force always ready to deal humanity setbacks, even in the midst of prosperity, spoke to Strindberg's own paranoid propensities and is closely related to his own theory of "the Powers." Linné's theory also fit in with Strindberg's return to a conception of God as a strict, punitive God.

Strindberg's return to God recalled him remarkably rapidly to artistic activity. He declared that God forbade him to indulge in scientific exploration and showed him that drama was his calling; quite suddenly, then, a lifelong dilemma was resolved. God, himself an artist, a conscious and meticulous creator of the universe, told him to be an artist, so the ethical and aesthetic instantly blended: it became a duty as well as a pleasure to write. He writes M. Jollivet-Castelot in 1898, "I have returned to the dramatic art in earnest; it is my profession, and I must no longer occupy myself with magic, forbidden by my religion" (*Letters* 13, 51). As miraculously as a phoenix rising out of its own ashes, Strindberg, who had for years seemed lost to the literary world, resurrected his career and embarked upon the greatest artistic period of his life; for almost the first time, he allowed himself to achieve his artistic potential. His marriage to the thirty-years-younger actress Harriet Bosse after his return to Stockholm in June of 1899 stimulated his creative spirit as well. The marriage soon failed, but the blissful early period of the marriage fueled his art.

Armed with his new concept of order and his new vision of dreamlike reality, Strindberg revolutionized drama by rejecting Aristotelean dramatic structure (of a clear beginning, middle, and end) and "realistic" character development. In these plays from the turn of the century, character and plot abandon old rules of cause and effect and take on a fluidity that destroys old boundaries and systems of order. We find this new world in the three parts of *To Damascus* (1888–1901) and in *A Dream Play,* among others. But fluidity does not mean chaos: Strindberg imposes new systems of order on these works. In the first part of *To Damascus,* for example, the pattern consists of a turning inward, then outward; the scenes of the second half mirror the first, and the play ends in the same place it started. As in *A Dream Play,* the characters move through stations, reminiscent of medieval morality plays; expressionists would soon appropriate these forms. Such experiments with order and its absence lie at the heart of *Word Play and Minor Art,* conceived and written at about the same time as these revolutionary plays. He also returned to interspersing verse into prose plays or even to writing verse plays, as he had done early in his career. At times, even when the plays are in prose, that prose tends to be stylized, for example in the three parts of *To Damascus* or in the 1901 play *Swan White;* like other plays from this time, they were inspired by Maeterlinck.[17] The verse sections in *A Dream Play* are representative of Strindberg's methods and purposes for interspersing verse in his prose plays from this time: the verse contains ontological musings and attempts to reach beyond the mundane to a more perfect world. Strindberg returns frequently in this period to themes and styles taken from fairy and folk tales, as he did earlier in his career in *Lucky-Per's Journey,* but now the forays into the world of fantasy are more metaphysical.

Alongside these plays, however, Strindberg wrote powerful realistic dramas, defying any attempt to categorize him and reminding us that he never altogether abandoned realism. The year 1898 saw the beginning of a remarkably productive period in Strindberg's career. Between 1898 and 1902, he wrote twenty plays, among them some of his greatest: *To Damascus, Gustav Vasa, The Dance of Death, A Dream Play.* But his unleashed creative talents flowed too quickly for the public to absorb; unstaged in Strindberg's coffers during these years lay *Gustaf Adolf,* both parts of *The Dance of Death, The Crown Bride, Swan White, A Dream Play, Kristina, Gustav III,* and *The Nightingale in Wittenberg.*[18] So, in 1902, Strindberg turned away from playwriting to produce a collection of tales called *Fair Haven and Foul Strand,* in which unobtrusively appeared the first version of *Word Play and Minor Art.*

Word Play and Minor Art

"Street Pictures" and "Cloud Pictures" illustrate Swedenborg's and Linné's influence on Strindberg; both poems make use of Swedenborg's theories of correspondences and of Linné's ideas of Nemesis Divina.

"Street Pictures" is an effective opening poem: it illustrates many of the new elements in his verse since his last venture into poetry thirteen years earlier. There is an air not of tranquility but of stillness in the poem, far removed from the nervous energy of the first four poems in *Sleepwalking Nights* yet not so defeatist as "The Awakening." The satirical tone is gone; understatement replaces polemics. The poetry in "Street Pictures" is stripped of all excess, all emotion; as a result, it resonates with implied depth. The personification of objects in the earlier poetry takes on a mystical dimension: all things share in the intense, inexplicable life-force that is a part of Strindberg's monistic view of life, and, in consequence, even the starkest details seem ominous. The realist's eye now picks up a surreal shimmer. As in "The Awakening," Strindberg has channeled paranoia into art. Now, however, there are no overtly phantasmagoric scenes, only implications that even in our tritest, quietest moments, we cannot escape dangers, powers, lurking everywhere. But all we see are houses, back lots, alleys, people sleeping. This new style illustrates the mystical connection between "mind and matter" that makes Strindberg consider himself "the Zola of the Occult."[19] The poem presents a hierarchical relationship between order and chaos. The basic level is the pathetic order man can impose on his own existence, the trappings of city life. The second level consists of those forces of chaos that wreak havoc with our daily lives, such as the Norns, despite that self-imposed order. These forces can in turn be counterbalanced by the higher forms of order found in nature and religion that offer solace to our souls. But beyond that will always remain something else, inscrutable and unpredictable, maybe good, maybe evil, where ultimate truth resides and where the balance between order and chaos, light and dark, is achieved, as the whirring dynamo suggests.

"Cloud Pictures" subtly reconfigures the neoromantic perspective of Strindberg's contemporaries. It begins with an apparently romantic scene: the contemplative speaker gazes toward the horizon at sunset. He examines the cloud formations, seeing in them castle ruins, "singers' contests, knightly sport," and the like. We know that the clouds are real and the images are not; they are "smoke and vapors in borrowed beauty." The poem sounds at first like many languorous fin-de-siècle poems, except for the speaker's exaggerated reaction to what he sees. Why does he consider the formations "dazzling deceit"? Because the stakes are higher: the romantic poet is satisfied with the creations of his imagination; Strindberg wants these imaginative creations to be manifestations of a real world beyond this one. Therefore, the knowledge that they are not, that they are only cloud formations, seems like a betrayal. Strindberg suffers from homesickness not for Sweden but for the world of the clouds, that Platonic and Swedenborgian world more real than our own.

A unique example of the nearly harmonious union of man, nature, and God in Strindberg's works is "The City Journey." Even the organist and his wife coexist peacefully: they alone reside in Strindberg's canon as the successfully married couple. Order prevails. Nature and humanity—the sun, the mill wheel, the smithy, the bees—participate in a daily orderly rhythm. And when the sabbath arrives, man and nature together prepare to worship the Creator. Even in a harmonious existence, however, chaos threatens to encroach. When the organist sits at his piano in "The Third Song," the music itself, even as it harmonizes with the universe, brings to his mind the injustices of existence on "this earth where nothing goes right, but all is distorted." The chaotic thoughts the music elicits inspire his dreams of a new order—a utopian vision probably inspired by Schopenhauer. Yet even as it threatens to destroy order with chaos, the music reaffirms order—such is its power.

We find the dramatist everywhere at work, and we follow the sweep of Strindberg's cinematographic eye. The opening passage serves as a stage direction, setting the scene; as the sun rises, we see the townsfolk preparing for the new day. These people do not face the day with trepidation as do the sleeping city dwellers in "Street Pictures"; they feel at one with nature and at peace with God. At center stage are the organist and his wife, and their conversation over coffee constitutes the first act. The poem resembles a domestic drama; whether it will turn into tragedy or comedy we do not yet know. In act 2, "The Second Song," the scene shifts to Stockholm, where the frantic bustle of Monksbridge Harbor contrasts with the quiet morning activities of the country. This is the kind of hectic scene, swarming with people, that Strindberg relishes, a thoroughly realistic scene, though mildly satirical, handled with great mastery and confidence. At center stage stands the organist on the fore deck, defending his crate in a parody of a Homeric heroic battle; the comedy even descends to farce as the organist and farmers scuffle on deck.[20] In "The Third Song," we are back at Årby, and once again calm and silence suffuse the scene, before the trappings of realism—"church mail with diocese newspapers, letters, certificates"—encroach. In this act, comedy and tragedy coexist and become intertwined until at last they reinforce each other. The organist's furtive trip to replace the old piano with a new one is comic. As he sits down at the new piano, the organist becomes a tragic figure mocked by his fate, by "the cynical frustrating life, / Which ridicules our sincerity," deprived of his fondest goal to become an artist. But as the music dies down, it becomes clear that at the moment of deepest despair, the organist has obtained his goal after all, for as he expresses his despair through the music, he achieves the artistic greatness that has eluded him. The tragedy, then, actually ensures the happy ending. The high comedy of the conclusion contrasts sharply with the low comedy of "The Second Song"; in fact, Strindberg offers us many levels of dramatic comedy in this poem. The result is a masterful blending of the tragic and comic, and of the exalted and mundane, that only an accomplished dramatist and poet could achieve.

By using traditional meter and nontraditional content, Strindberg revolutionizes the poetic form. The sustained Homeric dactylic hexameter in "The City Journey" illustrates Strindberg's freedom within the structured line. The poem describes now the mundane, now the grand, now the comic, now the tragic, with a resonant rhythm that never falters. The control in description is sustained in the dialogue; in a perfectly smooth transition, we hear the organist's simple words to his wife that reveal so much about him and that, despite the hexameter, sound perfectly natural and true to character. Slang and hexameter blend easily in this versatile poem. The organist exhorts his wife to "pinch our pennies," declaring, "I must now speak my mind without mincing my words any longer." "The City Journey" is a miraculous poem, Strindberg's greatest poetic achievement and among the greatest of all Swedish poems. "The City Journey" is the creation of a poet and dramatist at the height of his powers.

The poem-cycle "Holy Trinity Night" opens as a play; it in fact originated as a verse drama.[21] The stage is set for the presentations that follow: the main characters gather around a table at a little celebration in the local tap-room; we learn what each has done to greet the island's summer guests, and we are introduced to the characters. The cycle contains a tension between order and chaos reminiscent of works from other periods of Strindberg's career, but here that tension becomes central to form as well as to content and illustrates Strindberg's new monistic worldview of correspondences and portents, influenced by Swedenborg and Linné.

The first three songs as a group signal a gradual movement away from order. The Estate Clerk, who sings first, does what he can to create order in existence. He imposes an artificial order on nature, through his meticulous gardening, making perfect rows of all the right crops. His existence moves cyclically with the seasons and with the movements of summer guests from and to the city. In his profession, he even imposes an artificial order on death, making lists, sorting, and filing. This artificial order is benign enough, but it ties man to the earth. Firmly anchored in reality, he relishes all sensuous experiences; he tastes and smells all with unabashed pleasure. The Estate Clerk never questions the meaning of anything. Nothing diminishes his good humor: not rain, not heat, not even mosquitoes. With the Poet's song, "Chrysaëtos," love and chaos enter hand in hand. The Estate Clerk's meticulous routine vanishes in an instant, giving way to a world of madness, a ghoulish nature full of portent, where meaning often remains obscure. The cyclical progression of seasons is destroyed, as summer, autumn, and winter seem to exist simultaneously. Similarly, the fecundity of the previous section gives way to barren landscapes—autumn heaths, ice-covered lakes, a winter storm. The Estate Clerk's routine movements are followed by a feverish, pointless rushing about. The Accountant sings next, relating a dream "that I dreamed—at my desk." He tells the story of a cripple, miraculously cured by a woman's love, who ends up in even deeper misery as the couple starts arguing. In his song, we find chaos and order in open combat. The dreamer fills his life with a meaningless order, more tyrannical and paranoid than the Estate Clerk's, and more dangerous, for the Accountant tries to impose order on other people. He sees patterns everywhere—the notes on the sheet of music, the chessboard floor, the seashell staircase. He manipulates others with his need for order: he is disgusted with his lover's loose ribbon end, declaring "I desire your perfection, / And if I see a spot, I want to take it out." For this reason, boundaries between dream and reality blur: the Accountant's tyrannical need for order transmogrifies reality into nightmarish chaos. Here is the world Strindberg so often speaks of during these years, where reality seems like a dream, an illusion. The surreal has entered the poem.

Shortly before *Word Play and Minor Art* went to press, Strindberg decided to insert into "Holy Trinity Night" the two hexameter poems "The Rye is Smoking" and "The Meadow Barn," sung by the Rector from Skägga.[22] It appears Strindberg felt that "Holy Trinity Night," as he first conceived it, did not include a complete picture of his universe, and he added the two poems to fill the gaps. Both poems turn to nature for their subject matter, but not the nature the Estate Clerk describes, a nature manipulated by man, nor the Poet's nature, a nature distorted by a troubled mind, nor the Accountant's, a nature completely transmogrified. "The Rye is Smoking" depicts a monist's nature, a nature filled with Swedenborgian correspondences and Linnean natural mysticism. Close observation turns to monistic interpretation of what the eye sees, a sense of wonder at the inner significance and interconnectedness of all life. Strindberg combines the influences of Swedenborg and Linné with studies in botany and the occult in the presentation of *"Signatura rerum."* He has been criticized for dwelling too long on the scientific uses of weeds and making the poem too didactic.[23] But the botanical zeal and monism are crucial to his worldview. "The Meadow Barn" attempts that union between man and nature for which Strindberg always yearned, a desire that here goes beyond romantic transcendence to something more permanent. Sadness pervades the poem, despite its celebration of nature's wonders. The Rector lives with the knowledge that, as a human being, he will never be at one with nature; he will never live like the swallows underneath the meadow barn's eaves. He craves solitude, but he finds it unattainable.

The last two songs, the Postmaster's "The Vane Sings," and the Customs Collector's "The Nightingale's Song," view the relationship between order and chaos from a different angle. When these songs first appeared in 1902, the critics heaped abuse on Strindberg with some degree of relish. All the old accusations of incompetency with meter, smoldering since the appearance of *Poems* twenty years earlier, flared up. Tor Hedberg in *Svenska Dagbladet* called "The Vane Sings" "unbelievably pretentious trash."[24] When Strindberg retained the poems in the 1905 edition of *Word Play and Minor Art,* despite eager advice by many critics that he eliminate them, the cries of outrage returned. The critics did not ask why these poems were important. But indeed, in the world that Strindberg creates in "Holy Trinity Night," they are, despite their apparent nonsensical nature, the logical conclusion to the poetic cycle. They exist at the opposite end of the spectrum from the Estate Clerk's song, which celebrates the artificial patterns of man's social existence. These last two songs seem at first random, chaotic, but on closer observation, we find intimations of a higher cosmic order we can grasp but dimly. They illustrate Strindberg's belief that although events around us seem arbitrary or nonsensical, a higher system of order governs the universe. If we could but understand these patterns, we would learn ultimate truths about such matters as "sorrow and death," about which the vane sings.

In *Word Play and Minor Art,* Strindberg proves that he can simultaneously use traditional verse forms competently and freely experiment with new forms. This is perhaps the best measure of his maturation as a poet since he penned *Poems in Verse and Prose.* "Holy Trinity Night" offers a dazzling illustration of Strindberg's control over meter; the marriage of poet and dramatist evident in "Holy Trinity Night" is, in fact, mirrored in the poetic structure. As an illustration of his command of meter and his understanding of its dramatic potential (heretofore unexplained by other critics, who have not examined "Holy Trinity Night" as a cohesive whole), Strindberg juxtaposes the steady hexameter of "The City Journey" with a barrage of metrical variations in "Holy Trinity Night." The metrical variations reinforce the presentation of the struggle between order and chaos and reveal dramatic character.

All introductions to the songs and to the early conversations are in unrhymed dactylic hexameter, the mode of order and control. Early, we hear a song sung by the children outside, with alternating lines of iambic tetrameter and trimeter in a simple a-b-a-b rhyme, akin to a ballad stanza. Together with the hexameter of the introductions, this song sets up a norm against which all other meters in the cycle are measured.

In meter as well as in content, the first three songs form a group. The children's song is followed by the Estate Clerk's long song in hexameter, with only a few minor interruptions from the other characters. The Estate Clerk, anchored more than anyone to tangible reality, never wavers from a steady, predictable hexameter. The meter suits his tendency to drone on about food and holidays. It illustrates his love of routine. The Poet answers with his song of love—not the love of nature or food or entertainment but of woman. The poem has indeed entered a "minor key." The Estate Clerk sings of summer in what is almost a monotone; in "Chrysaëtos," we hear shrieking, howling, croaking. As we are thrown into the Poet's emotionally charged reality, we are treated to a barrage of metrical variations, regular when he remembers happy times, more complex and irregular when he rushes about nearly crazed by his loss. In stark contrast to "Chrysaëtos," the Accountant's entire song is in iambs. The sustained iambs are a brilliant contrast to the tortured rhythms of the previous section. At first, they lull us into a false security, but as they move on, unstoppable, they reinforce the claustrophobic, frustrated spirit of the poem. Place and time, waking and sleeping, all boundaries are blurred in the Accountant's song. The iambs also mirror the Accountant's own tyrannical insistence on routine in his daily life. Metrical regularity notwithstanding, we have moved yet another step away from the sunny reality of the Estate Clerk's song and the children's song, to which the Accountant's song responds in faint ironic echoes.

"The Rye is Smoking" and "The Meadow Barn" must be in hexameter, for they celebrate the harmonious interconnectedness of the universe. The hexameter signals that this is the part of the great logical universe that our senses can grasp. The verse and the message of these two songs differ from the Estate Clerk's. Although all three are in hexameter, Strindberg easily manipulates the meter on different levels of diction. The hexameter of the Estate Clerk's song is regular and correct but prosy. In "The Rye is Smoking" and "The Meadow Barn," the hexameter takes on a refinement, of which the Estate Clerk would never be capable, that is appropriate to the loftier tone of these poems. The Rector is a learned man who understands poetry and knows the tradition. He is a man of God, a thinker like the Poet, but one who derives serenity from religion, and his verse reflects the difference. The Rector's songs use assonance more extensively than does the Estate Clerk's song; alliteration, also prevalent, uses the more mellifluous consonants, above all, "m," "v," "s," and "h." Throughout this delicacy harsher sounds entwine themselves, for the Rector's ear, sensitive to the sounds of nature, picks up even its noisier elements. There is, for example, the corncrake with "the rankling clink of his rattle," "his creak and his squeak." Or the shrike, who "sheckles, scoffs, and quackles." Unlike the Rector, the Estate Clerk never listens; he is too busy talking and eating. The Rector's eye is also more sensitive than the Estate Clerk's. Finally, the Rector differs from the Estate Clerk in that he feels pain and despair, for he cannot control his world as the Estate Clerk can. Even a man of God can understand cosmic secrets only up to a point.

If we examine "The Vane Sings" and "The Nightingale's Song" in light of this discussion, they seem less like nonsense. "Holy Trinity Night" describes the attempt to move beyond the traditional boundaries of reality and language, to free oneself from the "vain artifice" of cultural and linguistic conventions. In these short final sections, Strindberg completes his journey through metrical variations and moves beyond the established limits of language. The weather vane, which "only sings straight to the point" and not nonsense as we might initially believe, speaks a kind of shorthand, the unhusked kernels of language unhampered by cultural trappings. As in "The Third Night" of *Sleepwalking Nights,* Strindberg seeks pure language. But here the intent is metaphysical, not polemical. In "The Vane Sings," the rhyme carries a significant message: it illustrates that indeed this poem is not chaotic. The poem's radical language contains patterns too—on this level as well, chaos and order coexist. The repetition of sounds that blend into real words suggests that a careful investigation of the world around us will reveal hidden meaning everywhere. "The Vane Sings" illustrates on the level of prosody Strindberg's theory of *"Signatura rerum."* "The Nightingale's Song" operates in similar ways. The challenge in this poem is to discern the tension between humor and tragedy in the sounds themselves and to realize that words and sounds can contain a multitude of messages, none of them easily defined. The meter is as meterless as possible, consisting of long strings of monosyllabic feet occasionally interrupted by quick iambs and anapests. Yet there is something compelling, something hauntingly lively about the song; it actually does make us feel that if we just listened with reverence, secrets would be told. The poem goes as far beyond traditional poetic sound and sense as possible. In the process of distilling the essence of language, Strindberg moves beyond words toward pure sound. But, again, not quite beyond meaning.

With a final assertion that, like God, another artist, he controls both order and chaos in this complete world he has created, Strindberg has the Poet end "Holy Trinity Night" by wishing everyone good morning in calm, polite hexameters. The night, the period of darkness and turmoil, is over, and the order of day once again suffuses the scene. People leave to go about their daily routines as the soothing hexameter resumes control. In the course of the poem, Strindberg illustrates what has happened to his old bifurcated character. Paradoxically, by fragmenting himself into several characters (all of them are essentially autobiographical), who on various and disparate levels participate in a monistic universe, Strindberg has achieved the only kind of harmony available to him, through refraction rather than unification.

Several poems in *Word Play and Minor Art* were inspired by Harriet Bosse, Strindberg's third wife, to whom he was married at this time. Perhaps the most interesting quality about the poems as a group is their clear illustration of the gulf between Strindberg's emotional and artistic maturity. He speaks of Bosse as he has always spoken of the women in his life: against his better judgment, he loves her and gives her his strength, seeking from her motherly as well as conjugal love; there is a brief period of bliss; she uses that strength to try to destroy him; damaged, he extricates himself in time to regain his strength, leaving her true evil exposed. Yet now he tells the same tale with greater lyrical and metrical control. "Chrysaëtos" and "I dreamed . . ." of "Holy Trinity Night" relate Strindberg's turmoil during and after the breakup with Bosse. "By the Outermost Cape" tells of his relationship with Bosse, too, but in more general terms, in a way that renders the poem more accessible to the reader; for one thing, it acknowledges the emotions of the woman, however fleetingly. It is one of Strindberg's most truly lyrical poems. As does "The City Journey," "By the Outermost Cape" celebrates the power of music to resonate with the cosmos—"all of nature has wakened and listens" to the woman's piano playing—but in a more intimate way. This poem delicately weds the monist and realist in its loving attention to nature's minutiae. The three parts of "The Dutchman" (part one originated, like "Holy Trinity Night," as a play fragment) trace the usual phases of Strindberg's relationships to women. Our heroic wanderer, here the mythical "Flying Dutchman," falls from grace, loves, and hates. The second section illustrates Strindberg's new monistic vision: the female body resonates with the universe in stately iambs. In the third part, however, the loved one is again "a little evil woman!"

"The Wolves Are Howling" contains experimentations with meter that are similar to those of "Holy Trinity Night." The first part of the poem sounds calm, but the violent vocabulary contrasts ironically with the meter, suggesting the calm is deceptive. To increase the dramatic intensity, the poem next moves into a sonorous iambic octameter that flows like a wide deep river. The city sleeps; all is still. This is not *Treuga Dei,* the peace of God, but the calm before the storm. We observe a delicate wisp of smoke, then realize its significance: "It's a fire! / It's a fire! It's a fire! It's a fire!" The anapestic repetitions break the bulwarks. The subsequent free verse, like the superficially nonsensical verse at the end of "Holy Trinity Night," is actually a logical continuation of the poem. As chaos ensues on the mountain, the poem relinquishes metrical control. It then settles back into iambs as the fire is extinguished and calm returns to the city, much as the Poet speaks in hexameter at the end of "Holy Trinity Night." But here the calm remains ominous: in the sky hovers "the picture of a black enormous hand."

Strindberg's perception of reality in *Word Play and Minor Art* is unique. Some elements of his poems are reminiscent of contemporary developments in poetry, but as when he produced *Poems in Verse Prose,* he remained remarkably removed from the literary tradition. He was more influenced by his own early writings[25] and by the work of early nineteenth-century romantic writers than by the work of his contemporaries.[26] He retained his own style and once again revolutionized the medium.

The poetic climate in Sweden when Strindberg wrote *Word Play and Minor Art* was quite different from that of *Poems.* The work of the neoromantic poets of the 1890s was vastly superior to that of the Signatures.[27] But Strindberg did not acknowledge much difference between the poetry of the Signatures and that of his contemporaries in the 1890s; his objections to the latter group read much like his condemnation of the first. During the first years of the twentieth century, he repeatedly lambasted the 1890s poets. Strindberg's objections stem in part from resentment at what he considered their denial of his own crucial role in ushering in a new age of poetry. As in the 1880s, Strindberg raged at not being considered a major poet, this time with significant justification. Although it is true that Strindberg far underestimated his contemporaries, it is also true that his contemporaries and subsequent critics have underestimated his stature as a poet. Like no one else, he created successful and revolutionary art out of his own psyche, converting neuroses and even psychoses into art, anticipating (and inspiring) both the expressionism and the surrealism that emerged in European literature a generation later. At the same time, his courageous retention of realism and insistence on concretion in even his most experimental works has kept generations of writers out of the abyss of triteness, vagueness, solipsism, and sentimentality. It is a mark of his rare brilliance and intensity that he must be considered at once the most subjective and the most objective poet of his time. *Word Play and Minor Art* is a significant achievement. Few volumes of poetry contain such a range of styles, subjects, or moods. Yet subtle thematic echoes create a haunting unity. In its many moments of beauty, in its boldness, in its general cohesiveness, *Word Play and Minor Art* is a remarkable and revolutionary work, which to this day has not received the appreciation or understanding from critics that it should. By virtue of this volume alone, Strindberg deserves to be considered one of the great Swedish poets of his generation.

Although he wrote a handful of short poems in the last years of his life, Strindberg produced no other volume of poetry after *Word Play and Minor Art*. He did return to verse in his last two plays, *Abu Casem's Slippers* (1908) and *The Great Highway* (1909). Both are in iambs. *The Great Highway,* in part a retrospective of his life, reveals how rigidly he adhered to his personal myth of the outcast until the end of his life, despite the titanic stature he enjoyed in Sweden in his last years. He penned these lines as an epitaph to his own life:

Here Ishmael rests, the son of Hagar,
Who once was known as Israel,
Because he had to fight his fight with God,
And would not end the battle until felled,
Defeated by almighty goodness.
Eternal One! I won't let go your hand,
Your heavy hand until you bless me!

O bless me, your humanity,
Who suffers, suffers from your gift of life!
Me first, who suffered most —
Who suffered most from pain
Of never being who I wished to be!
                        (SS 51, 100; SV 62, 210–211)

Strindberg's image of himself as God's rejected and chosen is there in his last work, as strong as in the writings from his youth.

To the end, Strindberg remained aloof, unallied, apart from the Swedish literary tradition. He was, nevertheless, a product of his time, almost a symbol of it. Perhaps one reason for Strindberg's explosive influence on Swedish literature—and on all literatures of the Western world—is that his personal conflicts coincided with the conflicts of the age itself. Because of his peculiar familial background, he felt like a transitional being at the same time that society itself was in transition to modernism, simultaneously rejecting and clinging to old systems of order. His personal anguish mirrored that of the age; it helped define the age. Strindberg's deeply personal, neurotic myth aligned itself to the neuroses of the period, and the personal and cultural merged to create one of the most remarkable of all literary careers.

A Note on the Translation

Translators seem to agree on only one point: there is no such thing as a perfect translation. Holding up a mirror to the original text and reflecting every detail of that text in the translation is impossible. Beyond that, disagreements are rife, especially on the subject of translating verse. Some believe adamantly in prose translations, arguing that the literal message is crucial and that a verse translation only leads to convolution and obfuscation. Others are equally fervent that translations retain meter and rhyme, positing that a poem is a song and that any adequate translation of a poem should be a song too. Both points of view have merit.

I wish to offer a third point of view: given that all we can do when translating verse is view the poem through a glass darkly, and given that a translator's only goal should be to make that glass through which we peer at the poem as clear as possible, the translator must decide what to do based only on the character of the poetry to be translated and not on preconceived theories. Some poetry may be so musical that a prose translation would be pointless. Some polemical poetry on the other hand may be quite adequately translated into prose. Adhering to this principle, I have made the following observations about August Strindberg's poetry: Strindberg was a remarkably polemical poet, especially early in his career. Though he wrote rhymed verse as a young man, he openly disdained the tyranny of meter and rhyme, arguing that the poem's literal message was of the greatest importance. But as he matured as a poet, he grew increasingly interested in rhythm and meter; in fact, a study of his experimentation with meter is essential to understanding his development as a poet and as a dramatist, as I have demonstrated. Rhyme was, throughout his career, of *comparatively* little importance to him. He rhymed in his early verse because he thought he was supposed to. Though Strindberg could dazzle with his control of rhyme as well as meter in *Word Play and Minor Art*, much of it is unrhymed, including Strindberg's greatest poem "The City Journey."

I have therefore concluded that in translating Strindberg's poetry the fairest representation of both letter and spirit is to retain the literal meaning and the meter while abandoning the rhyme. In one or two instances, I allow myself some license, for example, when I use iambs instead of trochees in "Saturday Evening," but these variations in no way obscure my presentation of the metrical development of Strindberg's poetry. This is not to say that abandoning the rhyme does not significantly alter the original; it does. The lack of rhyme in the translation radically changes the melody of the line. In addition, on rare occasions the rhyme is part of the message; in such instances, that part of the message is lost. But trying to obscure literal meaning in order to retain rhyme—which would inevitably happen—would not be playing fair with Strindberg's poetry. His literal message was too important to him. Abandoning rhyme in translating Strindberg's poetry is important for another reason: one of Strindberg's great innovations as a poet is the injection of prosiness, slang, and a remarkable terseness of phrasing into verse. Even early in his career, while still uncomfortable with the conventions of verse, he eschews convolution in favor of an astonishingly consistent prosaic syntax. The retention of rhyme would not give a translator enough freedom to bring the peculiarly Strindbergian syntax to light. Once again, in the unique case of Strindberg's poetry, rhyme is not as important. Once freed from the shackles of rhyme, a translator can with some fidelity reproduce the literal meaning, syntax, spirit, and meter of the original. In the same spirit of fidelity, I follow the *Collected Works* in retaining Strindberg's often idiosyncratic forms of punctuation and shifts in tense, since they well illustrate his mercurial nature. I have also taken some care to reproduce Strindberg's weaknesses as a poet in the early verse, including the appearance of filler words and awkward syntax when they are present in the original, as a way to better illustrate to the reader Strindberg's maturation as a poet.

Notes

1. *Sleepwalking Nights on Awake Days and Biographical,* trans. Arvid Paulson (New York: Law-Arts Publishers, Inc., 1978). Paulson's text is tamer than Strindberg's original, often avoiding Strindberg's racy language and compacted syntax. Paulson also occasionally omits lines.

2. Since the 1980s, Stockholm University has led a project to publish a National Edition of Strindberg's collected works (Uppsala: Almqvist & Wiksell Tryckeri), a projected one-hundred-volume edition, containing all his writings, including personal letters. To date, only fifty-eight volumes have been issued. I have therefore resorted to using the old fifty-five-volume standard edition, issued between 1912 and 1920, edited by John Landquist (Stockholm: Albert Bonniers Förlag). When I cite a work that has been reissued, I indicate a reference to that volume parenthetically alongside that reference to the old standard edition. I abbreviate Landquist's edition SS (Samlade skrifter, Collected Writings); I abbreviate the National Edition SV (Samlade verk, Collected Works). Parenthetical references to Strindberg's letters refer to the fifteen-volume *August Strindbergs brev* (August Strindberg's Letters), edited by Torsten Eklund (Lund: Berlingska Boktryckeriet, 1948–1976). Strindberg's verse has been reissued in the National Edition; I have based my translations on those texts. *Dikter på vers och prosa, Sömngångarnätter på vakna dagar, och Strödda tidiga dik-*

ter (Poems in Verse and Prose, Sleepwalking Nights on Awake Days, and Scattered Early Verse), vol. 15 (1995), is edited, with commentary, by James Spens. *Ordalek och småkonst och annan 1900-talslyrik* (Word Play and Minor Art and Other Twentieth Century Verse), vol. 51 (1989), is edited, with commentary, by Gunnar Ollén. All translations from the Swedish texts are my own commentary originally in Swedish.

3. As Strindberg explains in *The Son of a Servant,* he had access as a youth to the poems of the Swedish poets of the seventeenth century, of whom Georg Stiernhielm (1598–1692) was the most important figure, to the major Gustavian poets of the late eighteenth century, especially Carl Michael Bellman (1740–1795), and to the Swedish Romantic poets of the early nineteenth century—Johan Olof Wallin (1879–1839), P. D. A. Atterbom (1790–1855), Erik Gustaf Geijer (1783–1847), Esaias Tegnér (1782–1846), and Erik Johan Stagnelius (1793–1823). The only Swedish poet in whom we find a strong kinship to Strindberg is the eighteenth-century poet Carl Michael Bellman, although Strindberg, always anxious about acknowledging influence, never admitted it. But before Strindberg burst on the scene, only Bellman wrote of Stockholm in realistic tones. In the poem-cycle *Fredman's Epistles,* Bellman portrays life in Stockholm's taverns with a "realism [. . .] cushioned [. . .] by the graceful playfulness of a rococo world." (Alrik Gustafson, *A History of Swedish Literature* [Minneapolis: U of Minnesota P, 1961], 135). But he also saw a seamier side of Stockholm life, of drinking companions broken by sickness and poverty. Bellman wrote with a grace and delicacy Strindberg never approached in *Poems,* yet the toughness and candor of Bellman's vision proclaims their kinship. Strindberg also admits to reading the Finland-Swedish poet Johan Ludvig Runeberg's (1804–1877) *Fänrik Ståls sägner (The Tales of Ensign Stål)* in school; Runeberg likely inspired that combination of realism and romanticism and easy dialogue we find so often in Strindberg's verse.

4. Olof Lagercrantz, "Strindbergs satiriska och polemiska diktning mellan Röda rummet och utresan 1883" [unpublished monograph, Stockholm University Library], 12.

5. Martin Lamm, *August Strindberg,* vol. 1 (Stockholm: Albert Bonniers Förlag, 1940), 37.

6. Alrik Gustafson, *A History of Swedish Literature* (Minneapolis: U of Minnesota P, 1961), 254–55.

7. Olaus Petri, born Olof Petterson, in the sixteenth century almost single-handedly effected the conversion of Sweden from Catholicism to Protestantism. He was supported in this venture by King Gustav Vasa, who wanted access to the church's great wealth. Strindberg's play *Mäster Olof* (1872), his first great dramatic achievement and Sweden's first realistic play, takes as its subject matter the life of Olaus Petri.

8. In order to better illustrate Strindberg's growth as a poet, I present and discuss the poems in chronological order. In *Poems in Verse and Prose,* the sections appear in the following order: "Wound Fever," "High Summer," "Storms," "Youth and Ideals."

9. Olof Lagercrantz believes the poem was written in 1876 and completely revised in 1883, especially the first section, which "therefore fits in particularly poorly with the other sections" ("Strindbergs satiriska och polemiska diktning mellan Röda rummet och utresan 1883" 4). Henry Olsson brings forth evidence that sections II–VII were revised after 1878

and believes the first part was written in the 1880s, for it has an " '80's atmosphere" and a cynical tone Strindberg's writings from the 1870s do not contain. (*Från Wallin till Fröding: Studier i svensk adertonhundratalsdikt* [Stockholm: Hugo Gebers Förlag, 1939], 81). In "När skrevs 'Landsflykt?'" ("When Was 'Exile' Written?"), Teddy Brunius points out that Strindberg traveled to Paris in September 1883, when he had occasion to reflect on the earlier trip in 1876. Citing manuscripts as evidence, Brunius argues that the entire poem was written after 1882, positing that sections II–VII diverge in tone from section I because they are a pastiche of Heine's poetry and Strindberg's own verse from the 1870s. See Teddy Brunius, "Studier i August Strindbergs ungdomslyrik," *Samlaren* 33 (1952): 107–10.

10. James Spens, ed., *Dikter på vers och prosa och Sömngångarnätter på vakna dagar, August Strindberg's Collected Works*, vol. 15, (Stockholm: Norstedts, 1995), 322.

11. Quoted in Michael Meyer, *Strindberg: A Biography* (New York: Random House, 1985), 291.

12. Martin Lamm, *August Strindberg*, vol. 1, 193.

13. In the essay "Latin or Swedish?" from 1879, Strindberg argues:

[W]e had made a good start toward a national poetry [. . .] then they had to hire Roman gardeners, who cut off the young shoots. [. . .] To force the Swedish language, which does not recognize quantitative laws, into alcaic, sapphic, and similar verse forms, is madness. Did not the original Nordic Edda poetry instinctively take its natural form in this free verse characterized only by rising and falling, and made sonorous by alliteration? Does the folk song not advance by free *knittel* verse, where only the naturally accented syllable is counted, softened by the romantic musical rhymes? (SS 4, 258–59)

14. Quoted in Michael Meyer, *Strindberg: A Biography*, 125.

15. Olsson, *Från Wallin till Fröding*, 85.

16. Gunnar Brandell, *Strindberg in Inferno*, trans. Barry Jacobs (Cambridge, MA: Harvard UP, 1974), 247.

17. Martin Lamm, *August Strindberg*, vol. 2 (Stockholm: Albert Bonniers Förlag, 1942), 138.

18. This list of unproduced plays, as noted by the editors, appears in Letters 14, 200.

19. Evert Sprinchorn, "'The Zola of the Occult': Strindberg's Experimental Method," *Modern Drama* 17 (1974): 257. The French writer Émile Zola is a founder of naturalism.

20. In *Strindberg as a Modern Poet*, John Bellquist suggests that Strindberg used the epic genre in "The City Journey" to suit his new worldview and to blend the poem's comic and realistic elements: "a system of correspondences is germane to the genre itself, not only in the epic hero's continuous interrelationships with family, society, and the gods, but also in the concrete particularities of his world, which are interwoven, for example, in extended epic similes or in formulaic epithets." (*Strindberg as a Modern Poet: A Critical and Comparative Study* [Berkeley and Los Angeles: U of California P, 1986], 143).

21. See "Holy Trinity Night," note 1, in the notes to the poetry.

22. "The Rye is Smoking" was originally written in trimeter and tetrameter. (Gunnar Ollén, *Strindbergs nittonhundratalslyrik* (Stockholm: A. B. Seelig & Co., 1941), 173. Strindberg's revision of the poem into hexameter supports my thesis that verse form illustrates his worldview.

23. Ollén, 189.

24. Quoted in Ollén, p. 15. See Ollén, p. 16, for further negative reactions to the poems.

25. Martin Lamm, *August Strindberg*, vol. 1, 464.

26. Ollén, 108.

27. The major poets of the 1890s, according to standard literary history, were Verner von Heidenstam (1859–1940), Gustaf Fröding (1860–1911), Erik Axel Karlfeldt (1864–1931), and Oscar Levertin (1862–1906). The neoromantic poetry of the 1890s was, if not a rejection, at least a softening of the realistic poetry of the 1880s—of which, of course, Strindberg was a major poet. As so often occurs in literary history, the third generation offered a synthesis and a compromise between the poetry of the previous two generations: it was far more intelligent and vivid than the poetry of the Signatures (1870s) yet not so polemical or realistic as the poetry of the 1880s. In 1889, Verner von Heidenstam published the essay "Renaissance" criticizing the "cobbler realism" of the literature of the 1880s; it quickly became a handbook for the new generation of poets. Strindberg felt that Heidenstam's attack was aimed at him personally—in this instance, he was probably right—and consequently became ill-disposed toward the whole movement. Heidenstam, though less talented than Strindberg, was touted as his successor and the culminator of an art that Strindberg himself had initiated. Strindberg did not have to be paranoid to be offended. In a letter, dated 1894, to the Swedish painter Carl Larsson, he complains:

> I read recently in *Dagens Nyheter* [a Stockholm morning paper] that my ungrateful disciple Heidenstam called me "an old-fashioned prose author." [. . .] Prose! He who has learned new melodies from *Sleepwalking Nights* and perhaps read *Master Olof* in verse which has been performed at the Dramatic Theater. (*Letters* 9, 367)

Strindberg was temporarily swept up in the patriotic fervor of the turn of the century, and he genuinely shared the contemporary enthusiasm for folk song collection and imitation, to which both his poetry and his plays attest. This was, in fact, a life-long interest. But his poetry is always more terse and keenly observant than that of his contemporaries. Heidenstam and Levertin were both enamored of exotic, foreign scenes, which never interested Strindberg. Strindberg was much more apt to think of Sweden as an exotic place, though ultimately disillusioning, as "The Awakening" in *Sleepwalking Nights* illustrates. Levertin flirted with fin-de-siècle decadence. His poems are filled with languor; purple predominates. Karlfeldt was a robust, optimistic poet, writing mostly of folk life in his native province of Dalecarlia. He shared Strindberg's interest in folk life and folk songs; otherwise, no two poets could have been temperamentally more different. Only Fröding's poetry shows any kinship to Strindberg's. Fröding also experimented enthusiastically with meter, and he too battled insanity, a battle he ultimately lost. In my judgment, Strindberg's poetry is at least as vivid, compelling, and metrically sophisticated as that of his contemporaries, except Fröding's.

Poems in Verse and Prose

In Nyström's Studio

(Strindberg's note: Written 1869 when the author, at the time a medical student, amused himself by posing as a model for the work-in-progress of the Bellman statue, during which time he also created the rough draft of the dramatic trifle "In Rome".)

Number sixty Norrlandsgatan
Down by Humlegården Park,[1]
Where none but those needy devils
Forced to live on bread and fish
Go to seek their paltry lodgings—
There a little stone house stands
And of it I now will rhyme
A story from the year just passed.

Autumn with its blustery wetness
Had come early to our north.
Clouds not waterproof had sprinkled
Water on our humble earth;
Then appeared a young man walking
Toward that just mentioned house
As the clock was pealing four
And people started lighting lamps.
Silent he steps through the garden
Till he by a window stops
There he stands a moment thoughtful,
Leans toward the window pane,
Peers behind the paper curtain
To inspect the room within.

Can it be that thoughts of romance
Race around inside his brain?
Oh no! Amor's slaves would never
Go so early on patrol—

Now into the hall he saunters
Sniffing the tobacco smoke
Through the doorway next he stumbles
Throwing off his rain-drenched coat
Through the mud and sand he flounders
Lands at last upon a trunk.

What a muddle meets his eye there
Curious sorts of furniture
All to poverty attesting
And the trash is here in force.
Thoughts transport a man to Babel
When he gazes round this room;
There a bed-bench[2] stands so solid
But its base is badly warped;
There a chair on three legs hobbles
Leaning up against the wall
And above the mantle beckon
Kings displaying massive beards.
There a bucket full of water
On *The World of Beauty*[3] steps,
In a corner stands a top hat
By a sandwich half-consumed.
One finds also in the chaos
On a wooden bench some clay,
Next to it a man stands kneading,
Gazing fondly on his work.
Strands of hair cling to his brow,
The sweat pours down, his fists work on,
owl-like, huge, the eyes peer out
From underneath his tousled hair.
Now he finishes his poking
Wipes the clay off on his pants
And starts searching in his pocket

For the remnants of past wealth.
Finally, in spite of grumbling
Whining over trying times
After dawdling and much haggling
From the store they get some beer.

With much cheerful talk and laughter
Both drink from a single glass
Sing a ditty with each other
Nyström with a raspy bass
Proves himself a worthy singer
And with feeling he strikes up
"When I hear how birds are singing,"
He no longer can stay still.
Soon around the floor he dances
Till he's sated with that game
Then he pulls himself together
Steps up to his work again.

Often I repeat my visit
And with every trip I see
How the sun burns through the darkness
Bursting forth behind the clouds,
From within the clay's grey recess
Out the image slowly crawls
And into its lumps come streaming
Life, and truth, and pure delight.

See, there sits the minstrel fellow[4]
With his face well-known to all,
From the artist's head created,
He but waits upon the day
When he from the dead awakened
In a shiny suit of bronze

43

During heated flow of speeches
Round the punch bowl's cooling rim
Once again beneath the oak tree
In Djurgården's⁵ verdant grove
Might resume his versifying
At his lyre yet a while.

Brother Nyström then I'll sing far
Better than I now have done,
Loudly say to all the young that
One must never quickly run,
When to true art one aspires—
Unless you are content to harp on
Only old and well-worn strings.
You have starved and you have labored
You have struggled like a dog
Soon your pains will be rewarded
With a scholarship to Rome!

Sunset on the Sea

I lie on the hawser hole
Smoking "Five Blue Brothers"
And think about nothing.

The sea is green
So darkly absinthe-green;
It is bitter like magnesium chloride
And more salty than sodium chloride;
It is chaste like potassium iodide;
And oblivion, oblivion
Of great sins and great sorrows
Only the sea brings that,
And absinthe!
Oh, you green absinthe sea,
Oh, you tranquil absinthe oblivion,
Drug my senses
And let me fall asleep in peace
As once I fell asleep
Over an article in
Revue des deux Mondes!
Sweden lies like a smoke
Like the smoke from a Maduro-Havanna,
And the sun sits overhead
Like a half-lit cigar.
But around the horizon
The cliffs hang as red
As Bengal flames
And shine on our misery.

Indian Summer

From the sickroom's chloral-fragrant pillows
Darkened by stifled sighs
And as yet unheard blasphemies;
From the bedside table
Cluttered with medicine bottles
Prayer books and Heine,[1]
I stumbled out on the balcony
To look at the sea.
Shrouded in my flowered blanket
I let the October sun shine
On my yellow cheeks
And on a bottle of absinthe,
Green as the sea
Green as the spruce branches
On a snowy street
Where a funeral procession has passed.

The sea lay motionless,
And the wind slept—
As if nothing had happened!
Then came a moth,
A brown horrid moth
Which once was a caterpillar
But had crawled up
Out of a newly raked leaf pile
Tricked by the sun
If you please!

Shivering with cold
Or unfamiliarity,
He alit
On my flowered blanket.
And he chose among the roses
And aniline lilacs
The smallest and ugliest—
How can anyone be so stupid!

When the hour had passed
And I stood up
To go and turn in,
He still sat there
That stupid moth.
He had fulfilled his destiny
And was dead
The stupid bastard!

From "Exile"

(1876)

I

Agued Sunday afternoon lies dozing,
East winds send October clouds careering,
From the river empty seagulls clamor
Drizzling rain kneads street-dust into mire.

Jacob's[1] bells are ringing in the vespers,
At the holy racket ladies hasten
Seek advance on mercy for the season
Later they can sin with more decorum.

Beneath the opera house across from Jacob
Homeless bachelor in the pub sits puffing,
Anxious fever-flushed from last night's drinking
Flips through batches of the daily paper.

Outdoors laurels whisper in the rainfall
Laurels smoke stained punsch-besotted;[2]
Bloated organ music from the church floats
Through the panes bespattered by the street-grime.

When it harmonizes with the organ
Half-full punsch glass clinks upon the salver
Scaring up the waiter from his slumber
Bronze Beethoven glares upon the mantle.

Homeless bachelor sits sulky, surly,
Sees his image in the ceiling's mirrors
Yellow, ghostlike, parched, and muddled
Like a vision in a drunken nightmare.

Shrinks into the velvet armchair
On his clouded brow the cold sweat glistens
And the thorn embedded in his heart
Has caused the wound once more to fester.

Soon he dives into the paper
To forget through modern mischief
How his punctured heart still simmers
How the old wounds still torment him.

There he reads about great speeches,
Snuffed-out candles, lighted tallows,
Counterfeits and fancy murders,
Pretty talk and ugly thinking.

Of the bankruptcies and charters
Journalism by simple seamen
Homespun claims to erudition
Plays from France performed by Frenchmen.[3]

Jacob's church bells peal splenetic;
Now the sinners through the portal
Like a grey-black serpent slither
To the theater or ballroom.

In the pub they light the gaslamps
And the heavy blinds are lowered
Soon the punsch in glasses glistens
And the entrance door starts slamming.

He can smell the rain-wet leather,
Musty smoke floats to the ceiling,
Talk and noise and solemn pledges,
Bachelor alone sits silent.

Smoke-clouds hide the ceiling's mirrors
In the lamps the gas glows dimly
Loner's eyes pursue the smoke-clouds
Memories from the dead awaken.

Now he sees his home loom distant
Burgher home built in the 'twenties,
One progenitor a drayman
Who recalled the king's election.[4]

Worn mahogany, brass fittings
Double-bed dates to Carl Johan
Modest like a play of Lessing's
Dressers with protruding bellies.[5]

Lithographs adorn the parlor
Napoleon and Nikolaus
Geniuses like Torsslow, Högqvist,
From the smallest to the greatest.[6]

Out of massive oak the bookcase
With Franzén, Wallin, and Braun,
That time's taste: God's word with jesters,
With the seraphs stands a Faun.[7]

Cozy Sunday family evenings
Gather up the scattered siblings
Brothers leave their glad companions
Of the sisters none is missing.

Sees the old man smoking in his corner
Tapping to the music's rhythm
As the young ones try their talents
On the minuet by Haydn.

Mother walks among her family
Looking to the young musicians;
Haydn seems to torture uncle
As he falters at his board game.

Leaving seams and pins grandmother
Reads instead her book of sermons
She has put an end to dreaming,
Peers out on her world through glasses.

Home and Sunday evenings cozy
Happy sisters, cheerful brothers,
Poor man stares at smoke-filled visions,
In his brain the liquor smoulders.

Now the waiter throws a window open
Cozy visions with the smoke disperses
Out into the rain and night where wind-gusts
Can be heard complaining in the darkness.

High Summer in Winter

Outside winter evening blusters
Dark and quiet lies the street
Drafts the tile-stove damper rattle
And we hear the street gate clatter
When it wrestles with the wind.

Now the girl has cleared away
The remnants of our simple supper;
Let us light the candelabra
Night we'll temper with its daylight
Night was for our pleasure made!

I will go and draw the curtains
So the neighbor cannot see;
I'll pour wine in the decanter,
Seat yourself at the piano
Don your pretty sunshine face.

Sing of summer, sing of woodlands,
Most of all sing of the sea
Always predisposed to turmoil
Peevish friend, but ever faithful
Darkling depths and billows blue.

Nurtured by your cheerful singing
And piano harmonies
My geraniums are thriving
Born to live in torrid climates
Where they flourish into trees.

On your fire-screen regatta
White sails lean against blue hills;
On the stool the yarn-stitched cat sits
Purring on the cozy carpet;
Pallid flowers bloom again.

In the glass I see our little
Dwelling in perspective skewed
Though an optical illusion
Wine is not a feeble painter
Makes it seem reality.

Far away the work desk tarries
Under bulging rows of books,
Half-extinguished lamp smiles drowsy
At the black pen-points and holders
By a paper smudged with ink.

Then I look into your chamber
Light green armchair in cretonne;
I make out the household notebook
Sitting in your sewing basket
Mid the cardboard spools of thread.

Also through the door half-open
I can see your little head
Like a tempered blade your eye will
Parry blows but never counter
In the mirror smiles at me.

And I see your fair complexion
Turning pale the lamp's red beams
Flashes from your bosom's buckle
Throw a lightning bolt between two
Duelling eyes that blend to one.

Hush! The bell sounds in the hallway!
Ah I know well who it is
It's the mailman, last delivery;
As a mouse my dear be silent
Open not I beg of you!

Let them lie there in the mailbox
Hostile letters, galley proofs
Peace alone may with us linger
Mischief-makers both of them must
Stay inside the well-locked cage!

Sing to me my wedded mistress
Doorbells will no more disturb.
Sing again, let wine flow freely
Hours of pleasure soon will vanish
Until then the night is ours!

Saturday Evening

The wind subsides, a glassy stillness rules the bay,
The mill wheel slumbers, sailors furl their sails.
The oxen are released into the grassy field
All life prepares to greet the day of rest.

A flock of woodcocks flies above the trees,
The farm hand plays accordion by the barn.
The front-door stoop is swept, the yard is raked,
The vegetables are watered and the lilacs picked.

The children's dolls lie thrown in flower beds
Beneath the tulips' multicolored bells.
The ball has taken cover in the grass,
And in the water barrel lies the trumpet drowned.

The shutters are already latched
The locks secured, the bolts pulled to,
The wife herself blows out the final light
And soon the house slips into dreams.

In silent sleep the gentle June night lies
The yard's worn weather vane has stopped
But on the shore the sea is howling still;
It's nothing but the swells from last week's storms.

Loki's Curses

Our time's Gods, I who have cursed you
Come to curse you yet again!
Our time's Gods whom I have blasphemed,
Hear me blaspheme in a song!

You have power, I have language,
I have language in my power;
Thirteen you are at the table;
Signifying, as they say,
Death, destruction, great misfortune:
Gods, I want you to beware,
For the time is fast approaching:
Gods, I warn you, watch your backs!

It is true, I once was seated
At your table as a guest;
First you made me wear a blindfold
Then you dragged me to your feast.
That is why your foul transgressions
Loki understands so well!

Brimming bowls filled me with loathing,
In your wine I found no joy,
And your song, though fueled by feasting
Still was weak as kettle broth.
That is why, Gods, ye hate Loki
Who refused to sing your praise!

No, I will not sing your praises
Never serenade your feast,
No, I would much rather mock you
With my great and glorious hate!

On the rock you stretched my body,
And in ice prepared my grave
Once the little evil dwarf
Had cut my sinews from the bone.

Though you bound my hands together
And my feet in shackles forged;
Though my teeth have all been shattered
Free my tongue reviles you still.

I have dared betray your secret,
Gods, that was my only crime!
And my tongue could even reach you
Deep inside your castle keeps.

I betrayed your clever intrigues,
And your feigned holiness;
Never thought you were immortal
Knew your miracles were false.

That is why you mention Loki
First among your enemies;
He considers that an honor—
He betrayed those who betray!

When the meek the mighty punish,
Punishment is called revenge;
I have never worshiped violence,
Thus revenge I call my feat.

Good! I found revenge, ye Gods,
Hear that I have found revenge!
I have stripped you of your vestments,
Shown you in your nakedness!

I have scorned your worship service,
Cast your statues to the ground,
And the golden calf I slaughtered
Saw it crumble into dust.

I have torn the temple ramparts,
I have broken altar rails,
Bolted cages I unfastened
Rotten boards I toppled down.

I have found revenge, God Harlot,
All my youthful woe revenged,
Since you made me burn your incense
And you brought me to my knees!

When I came to sling the truth back
In your faces, pack of Gods,
Then I made your heaven totter
And your ancient fortress crack.

Idol vixens, idol doddards,
Frenzied you for shelter run,
Hitch up trousers, tie up dresses
Seek to cover withered sex.

Power seeks its battle lances,
Beauty reaches for the fig,
Virtue takes its golden armor,
Justice turns both blind and deaf.

Falsehood walks into the ditches
Captures vipers in the slime,
Ties them to the mountain's rubble
Where they spew in Loki's face.

And now Loki lies here fettered:
One against one hundred men,
Still the Gods in shameful chorus
Scream that Loki was unjust.

Fettered he lies on the rock-face
But his tongue has not been tied,
And the doddering old Gods still
Tremble when they hear him roar.

For through drawn-out nights of torment,
By his rocky bed his wife,
Shields him from the viper's venom,
Offers beaker's cooling balm.

But when wily vipers level
Their attacks against her breast,
Loki then gives up his scoffing,
And his voice roars like the storm.

When he shook his heavy shackles,
Through the rock the clamor rolled,
And in castles and in hovels
People fear the world's demise.

Loki then leaves off his cursing,
But from darkling half-shut eye
Lightning flashes, sizzles, singes,
When he calls out for his son.

Midgard serpent,[1] world destroyer
Rattles then his scaly skin,
Snake-tail stirred by world-devourer
Lashes by Volga's reaches wild.

Hear the rustling, hear the crashing
In Volhynia[2] forest's brush
And in Pyrenees the crackling,
Where his belly curls and twists.

With his breast he angry batters
Seine, an ancient holy stream,
From its shores you still hear whispers
Of redemption and of blood.[3]

Where the serpent's head lies buried,
Coward-Gods, you ask of me.
Future ever follows present,
When I speak your time is past.

For when his head upraises,
Gods, your time is at an end,
When you hear the serpent's hissing,
That will signal your demise!

Fire will the earth envelop,[4]
Burning all that must be burned,
Separating gold from glitter,
What deserves to live survives.

And the earth, once old and arid,
Now in fertile ashes clad
Has been purified by fire,
Breeds, creating life anew.

Then in ever verdant copses
Wanders free a newborn race,
Not deceived by Gods' caprices
Which ancestral spirits broke.

Then you Gods will all have perished,
Ancient feeble race of Gods;
You were fated for destruction,
Once you saw the serpent's head.

Standing by your black-draped coffins,
When your age has run its course,
Loki finds no tears inside him
Merely hope forever young.

He has offered you his curses,
Rudely spoiled your Godly rest,
To the One he still is faithful,
He could not believe in you.

By your graves these words are spoken,
Softly as if by a friend:
Our time's Gods, here you lie buried;
God Eternal still survives!

The Boulevard System

Where hovels once stood tightly squeezed
And blocked out daylight from each other
There came one day with pole and bar
A group of young folk gaily walking.

And soon on high
Rose dust and chaff,
When board and lath
They broke apart.

The rotten wood,
As dry as snuff,
It whirls about
With lime and rocks.

The pickaxe chopped
The crowbar broke
The wall fell down
From forceful thrust.

The scraper tore
The plier pinched,
The roof fell in
The chimney crashed.

From house to house
Their march goes on
From sill to ridge
All topples down.

An old man now comes walking by
And looks astonished at their razing.
He stops; appears to grow distressed,
When stepping in among the ruins.

"—What are you building here, my friend?
Will family dwellings soon appear here?"
"—We won't build anything again;
It's for the Boulevard we're clearing!"

"—Well! Our time's custom: *razing* homes!
But building them?—That is unheard of!"
"—We clear the way for light and air;
That certainly should be sufficient!"

The Epicure

Do you remember that old omnibus
Which used to shake along on wobbly wheels?
He once would wind his way up to the Locks[1]
But now he sits inside a distant shed.
The last old coachman, smarting still behind,
Lives on, although he teeters on the brink,
He sees with sorrow how each passing year
The owners of the new train company
Have been allowed to spread their tracks through town.
Well, I have known him many years now;
And when we meet we're always friends.
We met each other here last autumn,
I took the old man to the tavern
To offer him some solace since
His trade had just gone to the dogs.

I gave him cognac, really splendid
Which more than once has struck a fellow dumb,
The old man swallowed with a grimace
And only said: "Well, I'll be damned!"
He wanted me to find him quite an expert
And liked to think he knew his wines!

But then an middling-looking docker came
And also wished to give the man a tot.
He offered colored vodka though
And when the coachman came to give him thanks
The docker gave him porter mixed with strychnine.
That made the coachman smack his lips,
And with a haughty, knowing look
He whispered: "That's what I call real wine!"

For the Freedom of Thought

(November 6, 1882)[1]

I

The trumpeter buffs his trumpet again,
The master chef bustles about.
He cracks the lobsters and whisks the sauce
He stuffs the grouse to make them tender.
The royal marshal has fashioned a meal
Completely new, to honor the day
  The royal guard it proceeds to mount
  For here today we prepare a feast
    A feast for the freedom of thought.

The royal guard's guardsmen they play a chorale
From church steeples first thing at dawn
The banker locks up his bank for the day
The merchant dismisses his patron.
In schools they skip their prayers and texts
In shops they give up their salaries
  For this the Governor has decreed
  That all today have to celebrate
    A feast for the freedom of thought.

II

At Riddarholm Church there's a gala today
The soldiers are swarming about
And opera singers, ladies of every kind
Among detectives and dignitaries
The Archbishop makes a beautiful speech
The singers sing a beautiful hymn

And lieutenants white and lieutenants blue
They proudly believe that here they commit
   A feast for the freedom of thought.

As a final tribute to the dead King
They dedicate a new banner
They saw the sign but thought: just think
If only we could guess at its meaning!
Will ever a group, fearless though small[2]
That does not fear the cries of the crowd
   Be able to think thoughts together one day
   Without protection of rifle or stick
   At a feast for the freedom of thought!

III

In the chancel stands the reporter
And looks at the martyr's bust;
He thinks his thoughts so freely
But silent, such silent thoughts!

When his pen has tired of describing
The dresses and uniforms,
He cools his gaze in the side vaults
For the church it is rank with sweat.

The tortured eye comes to rest on
A trophy, blackened, unknown
Of banners in shades now faded
Enveloped in spider webs.

But there amid blackened bunting
Glows something as red as blood
As if the wounds though ancient
Had always continued to bleed.

For the group labeled number seven
He searches the catalogue:
"A silk banner colored crimson!"
It has to be that one there!

"In this flag"—the catalogue tells us—
"A royal ensign in shrouds
Through ardor for faith and doctrine
By infidel heroes was slain."

He thinks his thoughts so freely
But silent, such silent thoughts,
Today we know but one hero
One faith, one doctrine, one bust.

IV

At Norra Smedjegatan
Between two gloomy hotels
There lies so dark and lonely
The city's Catholic church.

Today there'll be no mass held
And even the door is locked
They have not held a Te Deum
Nor blown a Victoria.

Inside in the lady chapel
The warden bustles alone
He dusts off Mary's altar
As if he expected guests.

He then hears the windows rattle
From salvos and marching bands
"That stupid Swede," he reflected,
"He never changes a bit;

It's two hundred fifty years since
We killed their king in the war,
And we who had cause for rejoicing
Respected their need to grieve.

He battled against true doctrine,
He championed Luther's ragout
They celebrate that sectarian— — —
Ah ça! Mais c'est mauvais goût."

V

And chamberlains announce with courteous mien
That now the supper is served.
Here all are hosts and no one a guest
And no one here feels bashful.
A little *genever* with caviar
It raises spirits and saves the strength,
For the supper is truly impressive.
A heavenly salmon: Saumon à la Leipzig,
Teeming with oysters and lobsters.
An à la daube vraiment magnifique!
Chestnuts, morels, and mayonnaises,

Bordeaux and Burgundy, Rhine wine that fizzles,
The supper is splendid in Stockholm's palace,
And happy the man who was invited,
For he need never more live in fear
Of not being one of the holy horde.

You holy horde in battle dress
Where was your honor acquired
That you alone should arrive in a flock
And let your stomach tonight be ruined
By her majesty's cooks and his majesty's chef?
Today no one separates recruited from enlisted,
Although it is not inconceivable
That all of the holy horde was recruited.

But quiet the glittering trumpets blare;
The popping of corks can be heard in the distance
The holy horde now lower their forks
And dry the mustache in damask napkins.
They leave in the lurch a Boeuf à la Lützen
For silver necks have left the ice in the bucket,
Let trumpets resound through the banquet halls;
A glass of champagne to Gustav Adolf and freedom of faith!

— — — — — — — — — — — — — — — — — — — —

The speech is ended, the food is eaten;
One starts to search for one's coat.
Those nobler feelings must find an outlet,
One has to go to King Karl for a smoke!

VI

There sits a black-clad man in "The King"
And leafs through the radical papers.
His dress is civilian; but his posture reveals
That it was acquired in military parades.
He sits alone by the newspaper rack
And hears how they roar in the smoke and their cups,
About Gustav Adolf and Magdeburg[3] and Lützen
So grand and so splendid—and so new!
A portly captain of our recruited branch,
Who recently joined the historical society,
He loudly brags from here to there
About a newly hatched heretical view
Of the hero-king's holy history.
He whets his whistle with roasted chicory
And fuels his faith with a bottle of monk:[4]
"Attention, gentlemen"—after a swallow
He offers up irrefutable proof
That Gustav Adolf—now came from his belly
A nasty cough and his memory failed—
The historical barge was stuck in the mud,
For through the smoke he sees—and hiccups—
Two old familiar but burning eyes
And a sneer, just one, but colossal;
He saw that those ears weren't deaf to his words.
It was the civilian erstwhile comrade in arms
Who had not partaken of royal food.
They knew that he had not been invited
Because he refused to accept the new God.
He also was forced to resign his commission
Because he had broken regiment rules
By writing a certain historic tract,[5]
Which happened to touch on a sensitive issue.

He sat there alone with his wound and his sneer
And greatly disturbed the believers' cheer.
But he would have been like a fly in the ointment
If he at the supper had shown his face
He who would not accept the proper faith
And was jeeringly named in the jubilee toast.
And what business had he at that celebration,
He who agitated for religious freedom?

VII

The Catholic faith, that was the cause
The hero had in mind to battle
But so he would not seem the fool
He took some care to follow that time's customs.

He gathers thirty thousand men
All persons who were true believers
And every other one at least
With ardor burned for cause and honor.

Thus they advanced with slash and shot
And beat an endless bunch of Catholics
The Catholic cause resisted well
But Catholics they were defeated.

So for his faith he gave his life
But was allowed to keep his honor
And now the crowd walks to his grave
They hope to see the corpse make magic.

I know a man who for another faith
Held on to life but sacrificed his honor
The crowd will not be satisfied
Until his life is torn asunder.

It's not so hard to die in style
And mourned receive a royal funeral
No harder then to face the whip
And suffer life devoid of honor.

FROM
Sleepwalking Nights on Awake Days

The Third Night

Rambling about the whole day long
In a foggy autumnal Paris;
Startled, yes, but hardly bedazzled,
And admires in his own way.

Through the tunnels of brick and limestone
People jostle restlessly forward;
Like a broken mirror the street
Wet and sullied by mud and slime
Mirrors still small fragments of heaven,
Shows a picture, distorted and faint
Of the features of fallen man.
Starving people with hungry eyes
Jealous devour each others' food:
Wealth gives feeble hope to the poor,
Cobblestones make a paltry bread.

Loaded wagon rumbles and clatters,
Coachman's whip cracks like a gunshot,
Tramway bell whines out a warning,
Omnibus blasts its trumpet signal;
Trampled puppy whimpers and barks,
Clearance salesmen and journeymen,
Bawl out their songs with raspy voices,
Now he can hear a weeping child.
Always the mother tongue is the same
Mid the poor and amid the rich,
Always makes itself understood
By the Frenchman or Hottentot.
Why are you weeping, little stranger?
Does it hurt you, this sprawling city,
Where so many find happiness?

Ask, you asker! The answer drowns
In an alley where life turns musty
And where questions should not be asked.
Now again you hear banging and rattling,
Ringing, howling, hammering, rumbling,
Crying, laughing, whistling, and roaring,
And you stand there timid and wonder,
If you have landed in an asylum
Or the bottomless pit of despair.

Numb, bewildered, with burning brain
He flees the scene so that in peace
He can ponder what it all means,
And decide just what to believe.
Slowly he pushes off the main street,
But confused by the roar and din
Finds himself in a labyrinth.
Streets meander and alleys cross,
Gutters fill with the gushing rain,
Tired feet stumble and trip.
Wanders deeper into the thickets
Of umbrellas and overcoats,
He has lost all traces of cabs,
Ready to hang himself by his hair,
Hopeless peers at the gloomy sky.

Look, the alley is growing lighter,
Opening onto a boulevard;
In a grove of pitiful plane trees
Stands a church overlooked by the axe.
As in a desert when the Bedouin
Finds an oasis, spring-cool and green,
So to the wanderer feeling dejected

Mid the coffee houses and shops
Beckons the church of Gothic race.

Not to pray he enters that church,
Nor to adulate fetishes,
Merely to relish holy silence,
Loosen merely the heavy chain,
Leave behind him sorrow and woe.

Strolls a while to regard in silence
Airy ornaments carved in stone;
Wild beasts standing guard over flowers;
Holy men, whom the Mighty One sent
And the mighty murdered and burned,
Here they step on leopards and dragons,
For that faith that all things forsake
And the flame of love has ignited,
It can pass through the flames of hell,
Never asking whom pain avails . . .
Such things happen, such things have happened!
Upward burgeon the turret's stalks,
Upward gesture the speechless angels,
Upward the window's arc has stretched,
Upward the head of the arch stands bowed . . .

But inside he hears chinking and clinking
Through the window that stands ajar.
Hears he aright? A man is whistling!
And he smells something burning in there!
To the portal he hastens bewildered,
Cautiously opens and walks inside;
Mystical darkness reigns in the hall:
Colored light through the tiny panes.

But what abysmal clamor is this?
When compared to the din in here,
Screams and whistles, clatter and running,
The din in the street was nothing at all.

Are these visions? Has he gone astray?
The church turned into a factory!
Where they lay the graves of the dead
Now stands a water basin of concrete;
There a turbine with blades revolves,
There a hydraulic press pounds away;
Here the high pressure machine conducts
Steam in singing a song of praise
Glorifying electromagnets,
Which it spreads by the telephone.
And by electricity's light
Holy twilight is turned aside,
Then he sees that they use the church
As a museum for labor and crafts:
Arts et métiers are worshiped here,
This is a utilitarian's dream!
Look, here you have an emptied temple,
Gone are images and fetishes;
Everything carries the stamp of genius,
Usefulness has become prestigious.
Pardon me, do my eyes deceive me?
Inside a circle of slender pillars,
High on the chancel's seat of honor,
And on the altar's old foundation
Stands a statue of the lord of the house
With a rigid and stern expression,
Fully lit by electric lights—
The saint of this church is called Papin![1]

And to him they raise up their song,
Both the turbine and locomobile;
Pulleys, straps, flywheels, pistons,
All are singing in unison:
Hail Papin, and hail your cauldron!
This is your time, at least for now!
But the world will barely have praised you
Ere another will gain our sanction.
Soon you'll lie cast down in the dust,
Like those other saints of the past,
Edison soon might climb that hill
Where your statue so steady has stood.
You can still count on days of glory,
Still the cast-iron spire is yours,
Hail Papin, and hail your steam,
Lord of the world—but not of me!
Have you solved a single riddle?
Have you solaced even one heart?
Human beings are weeping still
Bloody breasts still bleed as before!
Did you make humanity better,
Are more people happier now?
Hearts you move no more than a log,
Nor can you open freedom's door!
Nor create virtue out of steam
Nor make bliss out of calories;
You have likely made many poor
When perhaps only one grew rich!

Very pretty and very clever,
Even the Devil will not deny it!
Nor do I consider it sinful,
That a church grew smaller again!

I do however deny that it's useful
Useful to all; but never mind . . .
We've arrived at the midday hour,
Darkness approaches, when no one knows!

Again the graceful arches resound
With a steam whistle's piercing shriek,
And to the dance round the golden calf
Steam pipes offer their organ music;
Coal smoke spews out incense offerings,
Gentlemen, how sweet a scent,
The waterwheel splashes its holy water,
Transmission belts loop endlessly on;
Just like serpents they slither and stretch
Never lulled by the water's roar;
Like that flame they say never dies
Burns the blue-white electric light.
Fire and water together press
Hissing, roaring the wild refrain;
Demon-like they all intone:
Ave, Steam! Ave, Papin!

Farewell then, church, you ancient relic
Of an age that bled and believed!
Now the new has broken the bulwarks,
Flows on the path, level and wide;
Nevertheless with a heavy heart
Our time's son advances through life,
As if walking a fire-scarred heath;
For the old, although it was rotten
It was vile—but what atmosphere!

★

Doubting spirit, always asking
Seething thought, flaming feeling,
Daily work will never deter you
Quilts of sleep will never calm you.
Spirit, again you enter the night
Thirsting spirit in search of water
Living water from the fountain of doubt,
Now where will you steer your steps?
You have burned two bridges behind you
By dismissing summarily
Both dominions of art and religion—
Narrow pastures and open ditches—
Out on the depths, the gloomy cold
Where you have seen so many fail;
Dive into knowledge, there lie the answers;
Books have not yet forsaken thought!

Once again I can smell your fragrance
Faithful friends through torment and joy
When I last downhearted forsook you
I was tired of your gloomy talk.
Now I come once again to question
And to start again at the start,
I want water from out of your wells,
I want to open mouths now shut
I want to slake my burning thirst;
Faith is great, but knowledge is greatest.

Here in the darkness I see your ranks
Follow each other column on column
Some are clad in a golden leather
Others clad in the humblest cloth;

Friend and enemy side by side,
Standing in armed neutrality
For the signal they arrogant wait
Eager to start those quarrels and battles
To defend what little each knows.

Come forward first, you black-clad guard
Theology, acquainted with God!
Never before you were slow to answer
And answered all with the ten commandments!
Tell me now, and don't mince your words
Your knowledge of heaven, your knowledge of earth,
Your knowledge of life, your knowledge of death!
Well, let's have it, you pillar of heaven!
Then a church father forward steps
A bulky quarto in heavy Cordovan
Dyed as black as the ace of spades,
And speaks of Christ, but more of the Devil;
Next comes another, and then a third
And when they all are talking at once
Then in the camp a great joy arises,
And psalters sing a well-known song;
And exegeses exegetize,
And catechisms catechize,
And bibles are spoken in ninety tongues,
Vulgate squabbles with Septuagint
Calvin and Luther fight with a cudgel
Gregory pulls out his *essentia qvinta*
And reads aloud out of the decretals,
And Arndt he passes around the morals
And Thomas Aquinas offers privation
Which tastes a little like rancid pastry
And Torquemada with tongs and racks

Exhibits faith's most beautiful products—
The final result is massive commotion,
Where he is beaten who will not believe,
And threatened with lightning and threatened with flame—
And abracadabra at last is the answer.
But that I knew very well already—
And pro forma is every degree
Preceded by a thorough grilling
And such a beginning makes such an end—

Now, philosophers, now it is your turn
You who have gone to the root of things
And never feared either Crozier or Skullcap
But stood in the way of fire-hot arrows
Of stalking theological hatred,
When seeking the truth, though you never found it!
You seekers of truth in wrinkled leather
Slender and thin with anemic blood;
Bad nutrition and meager honor,
Truth's reward to its champion.
Step away from the shelves and proclaim
How far down the road you have traveled,
What you have thought of the highest things
What you know that no one else knows!
Aristotle steps first in the ring
Leaning on life's reality
And you Plato who saw ideas
Where the others saw not a trace
Answer me both I dare to ask,
Where I came from and where I am bound?
Black the first one answers at once,
White the other promptly replies;
And when the answers are put together

One comes to rest on a field of grey.
But Socrates antiquity's wisest
Right from the first you have understood
Just how to hit the nail on the head;
Although you have warned us that in the end
We actually can know nothing at all,
They all the same keep piling it on:
One century argued it understood,
That being was only the corporeal
The other rummaged in the intangible,
And so the top has spun in circles
Varied occasionally by a few spirals.
What good to me what Bacon supposed,
What Cartesius doubted, what Locke understood.

What progress is Kant and his talk of pure reason
Since he denies us freedom and air?
And Fichte too with his precious ego,
And Hegel next with his endless nego,
And Schelling's absolute identity
And all the rest in a glorious heap.
If only two could have thought alike
Then maybe we might have dared to hope
But when all scream that they have found truth
Far better then to beat a retreat.
So there one stands in philosophy's mire
And ready to start once again at the start
The farther one goes the darker it gets,
And books do nothing to heal our wounds.

Jean Jacques I go with you into nature
To cry my tears at her comforting breast
Should Darwin count me among the higher beasts

That must in the end be my philosophical solace.
And come, Voltaire, come teach me to grin
When tears of doubt have been wiped away
And, Schopenhauer, when thoughts torment me
Hand me a needle with Buddha's morphine.

But dawn is breaking out there in the park
And morning breezes are slowly soughing
Among the frosty poplars and lindens;
And out on the frozen ground the snow
Glistens so blue-white and rosy-red
And there in the east a morning star
Pales with the blossoming beams of the sun.—
Here in the park I walked with pleasure[2]
Tired of books' eternal fuss;
Winds blew the dust from out of my eye
Giving my thoughts a healthier life.
Clusters of flowers on velvet lawns
Linden tree tops, buzzing bees
Starlings settling in nesting boxes
Jubilant cries of the children at play—
All things out there far better interpret
The richness of life and the meaning of life,
Than all the language in dusty books
Which only turned the heart into stone,
Which only calcified the brain,
Never made my spirit rejoice;
Offered only a moment's numbness,
Pointed the trail, as the dog for the hunter,
But never once could capture the prey;
Shone like will-o-the-wisps in the night;
Led the wanderer astray in the swamp,
Or pointed also too high in the sky;

Showed the way, but offered no ride,
Covered the eyes, and called let's go,
Often told a person to leapfrog
Where he could easily walk erect!

Well, then! What else remains to be said?
History I know all of your tricks!
You taught us to worship each common thief
Who managed to make a ruckus!
Law! When were you a lover of justice?
Most often you added weight to the burden,
You always came down on the side of success,
And dined at night with the sated!

Farewell then, books! You tree of knowledge!
Both good and evil you brought us!
Is that a reason to cut you down
Because you have spread out lies?
No, one day at the Final Judgment
Goats will be separated from sheep!
Then will, Morocco, your covers stand empty,
Which bear the marks of your crowned donor;
And overpriced paleotypes sold at auctions
They will end up in grocers' shops;
Then merely being a rarity
Will make no impression on truth's majesty;
The word will mean the same either way
Whether printed on paper or vellum.
Then maybe the last shall be the first
And what they used to toss in the flames
Perhaps will end up the most distinguished.
One day perhaps it will be your turn,
Who now are treated like paper waste

To lie under glass on exhibit days;
Newspapers then will be bound in calf,
And nameless greats no more will lament
That they were felled by the grocer's hand;
Then all will feel contentment and joy,
And all will hope for their own exaltation.

But of that moment and of that day
No person knows on our sinful earth;
And hope and believe, these two words
Have betrayed many a man.
And foolish prophet who prophesied wrong
Furtively slouches away from it all;
And so to avoid all needless quarrels
He thinks *in silence* like the Caliph Omar.[3]

The Awakening

Years of roaming have run their course
When tired spirit and ragged body
Long to turn homeward once again
To seek the places and memories,
Looming so fair for the homesick one
In nightly dreams, in poetry's daze,
To see if they stand the light of day
Without becoming critically thin
When the shade flies up and the lamp goes out
And the sleepwalker rudely from sleep is awakened!

Filled with impressions from Roma's hills,
Prussian tariffs and Swiss hotels,
Socialism and Septennate,[1]
Concordat[2] and eternal peace;
Weary of salads and sour wines
Sated with wurst and fake sardines
Macaroni, Hofbräu, and oils,
Danish cod and Norwegian haddock,
Tambourines and castanets,
Jingle-jangle and chansonnettes,
Boulevards laid with asphalt tiles,
Sun-scorched landscapes with veils of dust,
Dried-up rivers with beds of slime,
Meadows as red as coca mats
All that memory has collected
Colored corpse-blue by the sickly mind.
Now as the mallards' rallying troupe
Shows the way to his native soil;
When the beeches are starting to bud
Life-weary pilgrim travels north.

★

So he stands once again on the ridge
Where he often has stood in his dreams
Sees down there the river with seagulls
Ships and house tops, churches and castles.
All look the same and yet so different;
Never a dream came so beautifully true,
Colored by fantasy jewel-bedecked—
Reality surpasses the dream.
Spring sun shimmers on Gothic spires
And on newly built palace walls;
Wire curtains on telephone poles
Softly drape themselves over the city;
Green promenades on the avenues
Railway bridges' blackened planks;
Elevators, harbors, chausées
Panoramas, circus, museums,
All is magnificent splendid and new
Fairy tale has turned into truth.

Enraptured, proud of his ancestral city
Down he walks from his mountain perch,
Eager to look behind the façade,
See if the back wall is painted as well.
Rambling along the rows of houses,
Waiting to see a familiar face,
Now and then he searches his memory,
When he encounters a furtive glance,
Only new unfamiliar types
Slowly walk toward chapel and bank;
Stooping shoulders and faltering step
Lifeless eyes in a sallow skin.
If he sees in the swarming throng
An old friend, the man scurries off,

Turns his back on Heretic and danger
Pallid cheek and grey in his hair!
Poor old fellow has found a cure
Came too close to the black ones' net[3]
Lost his clients, his business was threatened,
Fell in the struggle for wife and children.

Weary, toward the tavern he hastens,
Gathering-place from long ago.
Rests a while at the usual table
Hoping to press at least one hand
Of the many he clasped in the past
During moments of mirth and candor,
Here where campaigns were formerly plotted,
Here where the beaker made its round
After victory, among true allies,
And where defeat was soon forgotten
Once debated from every angle,
Forgotten when the glasses were drained!
The clock ticks on in the empty tavern,
The sun shines through the tobacco haze,
Gloomy landscapes surround the room
Mountains black against heaven's fringe
Raise up hoary pine-covered ridges;
Silent waters sleep under cover
Of the moss-covered granite hillocks;
Slender birches in autumn rain
Weep for the summer already fled,
All too fast, like it never happened.
The clock ticks on in the empty tavern
No one arrives, time grows long,
Fretful mind seeks release from torment,
Desolation contracts the room.
Calls the waiter over to ask;

Starts to conduct an interview
Needn't torment the waiter long—
He knows all in a moment or two.
All are gone, the circle dispersed!
No one walks this way any more!
Gone from this life his oldest friend,
Died last year—he knows nothing more.
And another broken by illness,
Merely awaiting his final breath.
Old N. N.? Crippled by gout,
He no longer frequents this place!
One is married and stays at home,
One has taken up the blue ribbon,⁴
One has landed in prison's trap,
One has moved to a foreign land.
And the others?—They've disappeared!—
And "himself"?—When he mentioned his name—
(This had apparently made its way
Down to the man, but not his portrait.)
The man replied with a voice so knowing
As if the subject had eaten his bread
Or been someone especially sinful:
"Lord only knows, but *he* must be dead."

Quickly he swallowed the last of his drink
Drank to the dead, himself included,
His throat closed up, his vision turned blurry,
Eyes sink down into pallid flesh.
Out on the street he wanders again
Walking up steps in search of a friend
Ringing, knocking, trying the locks:
Long ago the friend moved away.
Comes by chance to familiar regions
Memories waken flash through his mind;

Shadowy powers dragged him there,
Thoughtful he stops by a well-known gate.
Squeezed among mansions a humble hovel
Lies there dark in a lonely alley
As among giants a little hunchback
Hides himself to avoid being seen.
There he one time fashioned his dwelling
Seeking to build a nest of his own
Into a home of his own he would walk
Out of the storm and discover peace.
Through the pane on the lowest level
Over a filthy and smoke-stained curtain
Between the bottles and cooking pots—
For it now has become a shop—
He attempts to paint for the eye
His former home in rosy-red hues
But he sees just a smoky den
Only hears drunken voices bellow.
All is waste, all devastation!
Where are witnesses, where the kinsmen,
Who one evening in this very room
Gazed at each other, clasping hands
To salute the young couple's union?
When in the wedding-hall at the banquet
Sparkling wine joined crackling wit
And they toasted to wedded bliss?
Two are dead! The rest have been wounded,
Gone beyond the Heretic's reach,
He who stayed to the last was the preacher,
Tell me, isn't that a bit strange!
All is gone, all have passed on,
Even the house was auctioned off
The storm arrived, capsizing the ship,

Dumping the cargo, no mercy shown!
Well what of it? The crew was saved,
The ship was protected by insurance,
The hull sprang a leak, the sheathing turned green
Nothing was lost and nothing gained.
Nothing lost! so the invoice says,
Then that must be the way it is
Well what of it, the stately mansion
Happiness most often disdains.
Since the foxes have their own dens— 5
Lovely dens in parenthesis—
Pound the street with your shabby soles,
Lay your head on a cobble stone;
Look about, any stone will do,
Or the alleys have their hotels,
Birds prepare their nests in the branches
Wolves lie down to sleep in their hides!
If you are sad, then shoot yourself,
Many had to settle for less,
And one man is as good as another,
He who can't bend will likely break.

One last glance he cast in the room
Through that window to where he once sat
At his work with a burning head,
Saw the streetlighter light the lamp,
Sat there still when night descended,
Out went the lamp and up he jumped.
There the lamp still stands on the sidewalk,
There is the pane and the room as well,
And the wallpaper, badly worn,
Is the same, but it hangs in tatters.
And he senses the bookshelves inside,

Pictures on walls, the dresser clock,
Memory quickly completes the scene,
There stands the table next to the window
And there sits a man at his writing
Holds the pen with a trembling hand,
Now he hears how it scratches the paper,
Stretches his head to look at the writing
But the sheets before him are blank
Long and white as the purest linen
No trace of ink appears on the page
The pen apparently moves in play
No he writes, he fancies he writes,
Look now he raises up one hand
As though wishing to give his thoughts
The living airy body of words,
Into the inkwell he eagerly dips—
Look now—he turns his face this way—
Dead man's eyes are as large as teacups
Staring darkly with sightless orbs,
As he nods toward well-known names
Pointing thoughtfully at his work,
From the depths of his throat he hiccups:
"Look, I'm starting to write in white!"

★

Lonely he walks on the folk-filled street,
Wanders homeless, enduring the shoves
Thinks he hears how people are speaking
Alien thoughts in foreign tongues
Comes upon guards in German helmets—
Guarding streets as if this were the Rhine,
Gloomy eyes underneath the hoods
Seek the shade of the market's trees.
Sees the mansions like Rhineland strongholds

Billionaire houses, *Berliner* style,
Towers and spires and steel-mesh cages
Window bars that defy the file
All is protected, solid and grand,
In the background a barracks stands.
Once again the homeland is mighty
Cured itself with iron and blood.[6]
Sees such numbers of new pagodas,
And young Bonzes with chic and style,[7]
Sashay about their idol statues
Practice enchantments and sorcery;
Instigate witch trials and prosecute freely
Excommunicate and imprison!
Still they hope to put out the sun
Light their fires with bolted flues.

The slime volcano has exploded[8]
Ashes rained from the mountain's mouth
The sunken city has been rebuilt[9]
Since we became the Persian's satrap.
Yes the barbarian has conquered again
Baltic Hellas has seen its grave,
There against Eastern hordes are stationed
Nordic guards by the Arctic Sea.[10]
This the end then to lengthy battles
To the factions and to the trials!
Discord has conquered, and step by step
Philip vanquished Demosthenes.
Troy is gone, we were the Trojans,
We have seen our Dybböl and Als[11]
We are known as Swedes and Lutherans,
But in fact we are nothing at all!

★

Homesick pilgrim begins to awaken
And for his longing has found a cure.
He can't miss what never existed;
Brushes the dust from off his feet.
Like the wise man who sought the ark
Against the wet blockade of the flood
Up the mountain into the wasteland
Out of the sinking city he flees.

Word Play and Minor Art

Street Pictures

1

Empty the street in morning twilight
Slithers, pushes into the distance,
Gropes its way along city blocks,
Cuts and crosses house lots and alleys . . .
Farthest, away in another quarter
Up it stretches, becomes a hill.
And there hovers the haze above:
Earth leaves off, heaven takes over.

Rows of houses, grey-brown walls,
Mouldings, drainpipes, balconies, railings,
Baker's pretzels and grocery brushes;[1]
Level sidewalk stones as margins,
Streetlight posts huddle together
Fence the roadway with iron rails.
The street itself a threadbare grungy
Carpet, brought out for a scrubbing.

Inside grey-brown walls lie sleeping
People awaiting gloomy fates.
Outside the gates the Norns[2] abide
To renew with the newborn day
Ghastly sporting with human lives.

Now, far off on the brow of the hill
Rises up a head that is moving,
And two hands wrapped around a cane—
Like a mirage it rises up,

And a man who sweeps in the street
Stands on the hill with his head in the clouds;
The broom scratches up a cloud of dust— — —
Earth and heaven meet in the clouds.

2

Dark stands the alley in autumn evening
People have left their windows ajar;
Autumn thoughts fill the stifling rooms,
Wistful sighs for the fickle summer,
Worry over impending winter
Questions about ensuing fates
Anxiousness presses on human breasts . . .
Houses breathe, the air in the alley
Stands in mist as if filled with pain.

But down there at the alley's entrance,
Looms the river with anchored ships,
Drying sails from the latest showers.
And beyond, on the other shore,
Verdant a tiny islet lies.

Uppermost in the crowns of trees
Sinking sun joins gold to green
But over *there,* and even higher
Hovers the smoke-blue city skyline
There is the sun, the cottages gleam,
There is the breeze, flapping the flags,
Highest of all is the church cupola
Crowned by a heavily gilded globe
Like the sun shines the globe, the earth,
Sending flashing beams all around— — —
But on the globe there stands a cross!

3

Dark the hill, dark the house—
Darkest though its basement dwelling—
Subterranean, no vents—
Cellar stoop is door and window—
And down there in deepest darkness,
Sits a whirring dynamo
Shooting sparks around the wheels;
Black and horrid, furtively
He grinds out light for all the region.

Cloud Pictures

The sky is covered;[1] the clouds career
Gossamer airships march with the wind;
All day long they may sail about,
But toward evening they join up
Gather the fleet in the western sky—
Rest in the lingering rays of the sun.
Now they stand up, dressed for games!
Now begins that mocking mirage;
Wanderer tricked by dazzling deceit,
Smoke and vapors in borrowed beauty.

*

Golden skies in the evening's glow
Fashion strongholds and castle ruins;
At the top of the red shale cliff
By a valley with small ravines,
Vineyard walls and peach tree groves,
Grand cathedrals and city halls,
Singers' contests, knightly sport
Rounded turrets on arcing bridges . . .
Now! Now the cloud changes its outline,
Red-scorched desert desolate stretches,
The Bedouin on his horse makes rounds,
Covers both the caravan's flanks.
There are palm trees and there an oasis,
There the camels and pyramids,
Gaze at themselves in water like glass . . .
Now, once again the picture glides
Glides and moves to another phase
Spreading outward, the cloud dissolves,

Gathers again at a kiss from the sun
Builds, paints, reshapes as before.

★

Land! It is land that I see,
When from the stormy ocean
Aimlessly drifting I fell,
Praying I'd find a grave.
Green-glowing shoreline, shade-giving alders,
Rocking reeds in the tranquil bays
Here I am home among equals
Here are my country, my valleys!

★

Island, my verdant island,
Bouquet in the ocean's wave!
Fragrant newly mown hay,
You I saw in my dream.
I saw in caressing meadows roaming
Light-clad children with flowing locks,
Singing and playing in motley flocks
Clasping each other in peace and love.

★

Friends and kinfolk I see
Hatred once parted our ways
No one remembers now
What occasioned our tears.[2]
Homesickness grips me, I want to go there,
Leave the crowded tedious earth
Torturing thoughts, insulting words— — —
Woe! They are clouds, they are merely air!

★

Clouds, ye children of heaven,
Stay in your soaring world!
Treading upon earth's filth
I'm never likely to fly!
Sometimes a black cloud comes sailing by
Tumbles down, and forms little pools;
Rain is clean but it soils the earth,
Heaven, though vast, is reflected in puddles—
Little blue mirrors cover the heath!

The City Journey

The First Song

Midsummer's eve arrives, when a single and flickering star sinks
Slowly to sleep below land and the East is colored bright orange;
All remains silent in nature; a holy slumber still governs
Creatures and plants; and in cottages' comfort behind the drawn curtains
People are resting, but ready to scramble awake with the sunlight.
Out on Lake Mälar as perfectly calm and smooth as a mirror
Seagulls awaken and quickly squawk themselves hoarse out of hunger;
Then from the land, from the aldercoast's white-polished stones
A snipe with a whistling and trilling sings his light-hearted verse;
The field-fare his castanettes raps in the riverbank's towering alders,
Deep within elder trees gurgles like spring-creek in well-polished stones
The willow-wren's masterful song; but nobody glimpses the singer.
Night has ended; a sliver of sun in the east rises up:
The fisherman pushes his rowboat from land with mud-covered oars;
The miller half-dressed with his hand on the lever raises the floodgate.
Noise soon surrounds him; the powerful mill-wheel starts clacking;
Gushing on root vaults and rubble the creek recovers its force;
The smith lights the fire in the forge and blows on the ash with his bellows;
Shortly the sledgehammer pounds, announcing the start of the work week.

                              ★

But at the home of the organist next to the stream by the road side,
Facing the church, which behind the stone wall shines lime-white and pristine
Newly arisen from bed the organist stands by the window;
Soaping his chin and his cheek and honing the knife on the leather,
Gazes around from his perch to see if the forecast that morning
Is to be trusted. That is important to him who must travel.
High in the gabled window he stands in his house made of timber;
Down underneath, by the sheltering wall, facing south, he has placed his
Bee-bench containing the beehives, half a dozen in number,
And the industrious insects already roam through the garden.

Always they start with a trip to the flower bed next to their dwelling:
Fritillaria, Peony, Columbine, and Adonis;
Then they go marching in troops to plunder the fields and the pastures . . .

Meanwhile however below him a window is opened a little;
Down in the parlor the organist's wife sets the table for coffee;
Places fresh blooms in a vase, and adorns the cloth with a border
Gracefully braided from leaves. Each detail proclaims it a feast-day.
Proudly she puts out her bread, the yellowest braids made with saffron
Cookies and pretzels and wafers, for at this moment the kettle
Leans on its edge in the hearth to clear the rich fragrant Java . . .
While she awaits her husband she potters, tidies, and bustles;
All round the room she conducts a tour on the freshly scrubbed floorboards,
Straightens the folds on the curtain of flowered taffeta cotton,
Picks off a withering leaf from the balsamine in the window,
And with the dust rag she briefly flies over the aging piano
In its now faded shell made of cedar, or so-called mahogany
Dusting the keyboard and its delicate keys very gently;
Hammers of quill-pen needles which tap against strings made of brass
It sounds like a Spanish guitar, with its brittle and delicate chinking.—

Time has been shuffling along and trials of today have muted
Notes from the springtime of youth, for one now has arrived at age forty.
Then the door opens, the man of the house enters dressed for the city;
In a black frock-coat and wearing a self-tied many-hued kerchief
Lending a youthful sheen to a shiny and newly shaved visage;
Nods to his pottering wife in a friendly greeting and tells her:
"Well then, my dear, on this day twenty years ago our wedding
Here in this village was held, and it cheers me to find you remember,
Cheers me to see that with festive board you observe this occasion.
Hardship and toil filled our life, in the fields, in the school, in the church, too;
Many small mouths we have fed, when grain and harvest were meager.
Always with concord and song, with good-natured hearts we have pulled

The burden halfway to the end; now the downhill journey awaits us.
Therefore, my wife, we must ever more tightly pinch our pennies;
For our children grow quickly, requiring greater expenses,
Yes, I must now speak my mind without mincing my words any longer:
Greed *is* a virtue for him whose house contains plenty of children—
I have grown greedy, I also; so starting this day and this hour
I do not want on our table gentleman's food or belongings . . .
Rye is the poor man's diet, and wheat should be left to the wealthy—
Unblended coffee is fine for counts and elegant barons,
Half of Brazilian, half of Java the choice of the vicar,
But a poor man like the Årby organist should select barley,
Barley quite lightly roasted, a smidgeon of chickory, *nec ultra*.
Now then, my dear, you know how I wish you to manage the household.
Nary a word from now on will I speak of this troublesome matter—
Hope you have well understood, do not be upset by these trifles."

Silent and still stood his wife, unhappy, defeated, and speechless;
Never before such a tone and such words had she heard from her husband;
Nor had she ever suspected that such was the household's condition,
Rather she hoped and believed that the bank was collecting a surplus.
This was to be the reward, then, for hardships and frugal housekeeping:
Starting restrictions and miserliness with old age approaching!—
Glad and contented her husband appeared that his words hit their target;
But then he furtively smiled and bent his head over his coffee,
Spoke friendly words to his wife, and quietly joked as he used to.
Finishing breakfast he patted his wife on the cheek as he thanked her;
Rose to his feet, walked into the parlor and as if at random,
Or just to tease her, perhaps, struck a chord upon the piano—
"Still it sounds perfectly tuned," that humorous organist said,
"The tone is still strong and not one of the strings in the box is yet missing;
All our lives it may last, and the children's too, for that matter."
Speaking he reached for his hat, for the steamer horn blew in the inlet,
Nodded a friendly farewell and hastened out through the doorway.

The Second Song

Riddarholm Church chimes three, and the German Church promptly responds;
The Lake Mälar steamer casts off from the teeming harbor at Monksbridge;[1]
Billows and steams, then reverses; the gangway is swarming with people;
Stowing his cargo the first mate answers answerless questions;
Deck-hands maneuver their lines; at the helm the captain stands waiting
Under a roof made of birch-leaves, but peonies hang from the fo'c'sle
No doubt to honor the day, for midsummer's eve has arrived.
The steamer now wobbles away from the waving throng in the harbor
Bright-colored maypoles surround the leafmerchant's [2] many-hued sales
    booth,
Meanwhile the spirited concert of fiddles, trumpets, and woodwinds
Drowns and is silenced to death by the steamers' whistling and ringing.
But on a fore-deck on board the leaf-adorned Lake Mälar ship
The organist looms surrounded by tipsy farmers and cargo.
Towering over the crowd he stands guarding a crate with his fists raised,
Long as a door and as wide as a double bed at the far end;
All round the crate stands a fortress of baskets, cages, and boxes,
Like a besieging army the tipsy farmers press round him
Seeking a seat on the crate, but the organist warlike defends it.
Here he delivers a shove to backs dressed in homespun jerkin,
There with his foot he deposits a boot on tottering knee joints;
And when the hostile horde considers his treasure a sofa,
Pressed into cuffing and face-slaps, and more, with brute force he defends
His ownership rights against people who only listen when fists talk.
"Winning (he thinks to himself) is nothing compared to defending;
Life will give nothing for nothing, and all must be taken and stolen;
Heaven itself must be conquered by force! Well come on, taste my fists, then!"
Suffering organist sweats in the sun beating down without mercy;
Smoke from the fo'c'sle and kitchen and tallow from laboring engine
Stir up the fiery warrior who traded battle for word-war.
Hunger besets him, and out of the restaurant doorway
Rises a ravishing smell of simmering beef-steak in soy sauce.
But at his post he maintains loyal guard and reflects it is sweet

To suffer defending one's own.—The blue bay now stretches before them;
The wind blows across the beam as the steamer veers off to leeward;
There you see Mälarestrand[3] in midsummer's fullest perfection;
Heaven is wedded to earth, one can scarcely keep them asunder
Heaven is blue, but the water is bluer, the faraway woodland
Looks like the firmament's sky, and the sky resembles a woodland;
Green-glowing islands and skerries attired with trees in their leafing
Right between water and air, one knows not in what realm they belong;
The air is warm, but not hot; is fresh, but not cold; and one moves
As if in warm rooms, where the windows stand open to let in the sunshine.
Look now, what beautiful pictures approach and recede from our vision:
Here first a shoreline emerges where timber-pines cover the hillside,
Followed by sandpits frequented by well-known half-open freighters;
There one sees glimmering fields of rye and the gold-yellow mustard;
Marsh-meadows barren and wet with cabbage-reeds down in the water;
Here by a spit emerges a brick-works' mud-grey encampment;
Hills now take over the shoreline; and promptly a mill he steps forward
Eagerly seeking a bath in the gurgling creek with his mill wheel.
Slowly the bay contracts itself into a strait and a manor
White as newly cut lime, on the roof a belfry with flagpole;
Next to the steamboat pier lies the rosy-red bath house at anchor;
Down to the shore runs the garden, a paradise laden with fruit trees,
None is forbidden fruit, and snakes never lurk in the grass here;
Gooseberry thickets in rows and raspberry forests abounding— — —
And so the splendor has passed, the stony alder-shore follows:
Alders and stones and stones and alders; a strutting wag-tail
Chirrups farewell on the headland, and into the bay steers the steamer!
Grebes sail about close at hand; a sweeping crow and a seagull;
Otherwise all things are dead on the wide-open water an hour,
Far away smoke from a steamer proclaims the civilized regions,
Coming perhaps from a city, a summer home, or a manor;
Lake Mälar teems with estates, not only historical memories
Precious to Upswedish men.[4] Name Sture and Oxenstierna,
Vasa and Brahe, Banér; the rest need not even be mentioned.[5]

Tynnelsö, Rävsnäs, Gripsholm, with Tidö, Svartsjö, and Kungsör,[6]
Pictures of Sweden's bold history are passing before you.

— — — — —

Now in the blue-white air to the steamer's windward come stretching
Swans in magnificent pairs; they steer toward wonderful Ekoln,
To the worn wanderer on fore-deck a sign that his own coast approaches.

The Third Song

High summer calm reigns in air and in leaves, on the lands, in the water;
Silence prevails on our earth, for Sunday peace holds dominion,
When from the bell-tower's perch the church-bells have rung in the Sabbath.
The mill-wheel has stopped, and the stagnating stream seeps away in the
    stream-bed;
Draught horses rest in their cribs and their stalls relieved of their harness.
Children relate having noticed the bees staying inside the bee-hive,
Birds sit on branches preparing for worship with painstaking preening;
Fishes have sought out the deep, no longer engaged in their play
The grasshopper keeps to himself in subterranean chambers—
Never a snake has been sighted on Sunday mornings, and never
Buzzard or hawk; the swallow himself under swaying steeple
Tremulous clings to his hold when the powerful bells begin pealing.
This day belongs to our Lord and the house of our Lord it stands open;
Largest that house in the village, the handsomest too in the parish . . .
White as the wing of a dove and arched like the great dome of heaven,
Ceiling so high it appears to be built for gods, or for giants.
A forest of pillars holds up the towering vaults, at the bottom
Dragons and trolls they trample just as the roots of the World-Tree[7]
Trample that ancient snake, destroyer, All-gnawer Nidhögg.[8]
But round the holy house, the shimmering white, there the Dead Ones'
Flowering garden is laid out in beds well measured and verdant
Labeled with poles and with crosses, telling of names half forgotten
Looking somewhat like a tree farm with trees in parallel columns . . .
This is heaven's herb garden; they slumber, reshape, grow again.

The bells begin pealing anew, for a second time; at their urging
Slowly the spacious church starts to fill up with gaily dressed people.
Silent the verger on tip-toe posts the hymns for the service;
Here comes the organ blower; he walks up the creaking loft stair,
Dusts off the organ and pulls out a stop from a well-filled selection
Chooses the sixteen-foot principal; always the bass is the clincher,
Serves as a safety-valve too, protecting the over-filled bellows.
Meanwhile the organist comes from the sacristy and the rector,
Leaving his church mail with diocese newspapers, letters, certificates,
Baptisms, church banns, and bills, surveyors' fees, proclamations.
Now he walks up to his seat between the columns of church pews,
Furtively nods to his wife next to the assessor's widow,
Reaches his lofty seat; and in front of the Haeffner hymnal
Sits himself down and pulls out the stops, then begins the preludium
Of our Sebastian Bach, the greatest who played on the organ;
Singer of torment and woe, requiring one hundred voices,
Amply the organ responds, and the mighty lungs of the bellows . . .
Does it not seem to you that the blower engaged at the organ
Places his ponderous foot on the breast of the vanquished Titan?
Now the Processional sounds and the high mass service commences
All goes according to plan; one arrives at the start of the sermon— — —
Then with dispatch the talented organist sneaking on tip-toe
Creeps down the stairs. They creak and complain as if wishing to tattle.—
Soon he arrives at the porch, and moves past its hoses and buckets;
Meets in the church yard his bell ringers, four reliable fellows.
Planned it appears to be, now they whisper in secret communion,
Then to the organist's home in a half-trot they quietly hasten.
Well, then what happened? Some vigilant boys will later relate
That out of the house was carried, covered with newly washed sail-cloth
Something resembling a beast with legs sticking straight toward heaven,
And that this something was spirited off pell-mell to the hayloft.
Later—the story continues—an even larger contraption
Back from the hayloft was carried, and at a jolt in the hall-way

Rumbled and crashed like a music box dog one can buy at the market.

————————

Amen has sounded; the sermon and altar service are over;
Reaching his seat the organist picks the recessional music,
When he has chosen, with no stops barred he engages his organ;
Mendelssohn's wedding march from the Midsummer's Dream he commences,
Festive and pompous, not lacking a certain intention;
And when he looks in the mirror, a gaze from his wife he encounters
Questioning, giving an answer, she then disappears in the jumble.
All is complete; when the doors have shut to the leaf-adorned temple,
Homeward the organist rushes; a head start now is essential;
He knows quite well that his wife an errand must run to the parson's;
All is arranged, worked out in advance, and cannot misfire.

So the contented organist entered the feast-readied parlor,
Throws down his hat and opens the glistening walnut piano,
Strikes a few chords and slides into a run, he rolls through the octaves;
Finds himself inside a theme, his hands are brimming with music;
And from the depths of the "supine harp" a majestic toccata
By our Sebastian Bach, his foremost teacher, emerges;
And it translates his life into tormented, thundering rhythms:
Dreams from his youth about Art, the great and glorious Calling,
Which for his home and his hearth, for his bread he was forced to relinquish;
Memories come crowding in; he envisions himself as a young man,
Hands were still white then, not burned by the sun from seasons of tilling,
At the academy once, in the capital he made a promise
To live a brilliant life, devoted in earnest to music
And at a concert in Klara Church he performed on the organ;
That same toccata he on the piano just called up from memory.
In the piano's veneer he saw how his hands were reflected
Massive and hairy and stiff, the knuckles swollen by frost-bite.
He grew ashamed of touching the ivory keys with such roughness,
Delicate, smooth, far better suited to woman's caresses . . .
Finally he reawakens; he feels as if life has betrayed him,

Seized by a holy anger, by wrath and a furious anguish;
Plays a few minor chords, then suddenly throws himself into
Beethoven's greatest sonata, the titanic Appassionata . . .
Now like a lion, which batters his cage with blood-covered paws
He charges out onto the keyboard and grapples in every direction . . .
Powerful fists are hammered fast to the steel-string piano,
Feet nailed down on the pedals a crucified man he resembles.
All that is bitter in life, the cynical frustrating life,
Which ridicules our sincerity, mocks our holy emotions
Calling for duty and sacrifice, then that sacrifice jeering;
Life takes our pitiful fate, turns it into a scourge upon us,
Makes us torment our most dearly beloved, to wound and to chastise,— — —
Thus the sonata develops, the wordless, powerful poem,
Roars and bewails with an impotent wrath the pain of existence.
"What has become of the sacred promise of peace on our earth?
Human intentions are noble, peace is our greatest desire;
Forced into violence and war, to betrayal and treacherous language—
Harken to roars of the damned who have lost all their faith in goodness;
Life is ugly, an evil, yet people abominate evil.
Does he not suffer who sevenfold battered the already conquered?⁹
Mankind's intentions were good, but life insisted on evil.
Now you can hear the prisoners' shrieks from their earthly prison;
Over their heads they see blue, and imagine at once it is heaven;
Reach them a friendly hand, and they think it belongs to an angel;
All men in goodness believe; then why do we label them evil?
Woe! this earth where nothing goes right, but all is distorted.
Faith turns to doubt, and sowing in love means reaping in hatred;
Though you have planted your hope, despair is the fruit you must harvest
Let Ragnarök,¹⁰ world-burning, the death of the gods, be upon us.
Next let the deluge arrive, a cleansing with fire and water;
Thus we can start once again, in the fertile ooze and the ashes
Tilling and sowing. The golden age of our dreams then approaches."
— — — — — — —
The music has come to an end, but the strings continue to chime

Like echoes from out of the past, an answer from harmonized spirits.
Also benumbed he sat silent, amazed at his magical powers,
Although the humble parlor it trembled still from the thunder,
Peals of a thunder brought forth by the conjurer without his knowledge.
Outside the open window he heard a resounding "bravo,"
Followed by eager applause from a number of hands; it felt so
Friendly and soft and so warm as if someone his cheek were caressing.
Quickly he rose from his seat and saw through the open window
Sitting inside their magnificent carriage the Count's noble family . . .
There stood the Dean next to them with his sons, his daughters, their
   husbands
Once more they raised up a cheer and the organist stepped forward
   bowing.—
Then in a moment he felt how all his bitterness vanished;
Life smiled again; for one second he relished the triumph of artists;
Spirits and hearts he ignited, compelling the masters to listen.

Now turning into the room he could feel a hand on his shoulder;
There stood his wife, and quite touched by the tribute accorded her husband
Did not know how with expression and gesture she should address him;
Taking her husband's hand into hers she forcefully pressed it
Happy to find once again the man she had feared lost forever . . .
Both were delighted as children to look at the gleaming piano
Wages for years of labor, a force that entered the household.
Also it beamed out a power, it cast a glow all around them
Shone on the paltry furnishings, elevated the humble.
Marveling over the scene, the villagers peered through the windows—
Then at a wink the children came running and happiness greater
Than they had ever encountered filled the poor organist's homestead.

Holy Trinity Night

The taproom at Fagervik[1] in the evening. The interior windows upstage are removed and the glass doors to the verandah are opened.

The Customs Collector, the Pilot Master, and the Postmaster sit at a table drinking.

THE CUSTOMS COLLECTOR

Spring has arrived! Like the waves broke the ice let us break out the windows!
Let out the winter air, make the stove stand there cold in his corner.[2]
Sallow and wind-flowers, springtime and youth at the door wait to greet us;
Dear Mrs. Lundström put vodka on ice and prepare a light supper,
Supper[3] for seven with crayfish and eel and also new radishes;
Don't forget Burträsk cheese and the tender Bergmanian crispbread;
Next you must fill up the jugs with the foaming Saint Erik's Pilsener,
Then take the porter and mix it one part to two with the Pilsener;
That is a banquet prepared in a true Swedish way—I have spoken!

THE POSTMASTER

Well you have spoken my friend and customs-collecting brother;
Food for the body is fine, but the spirit must also be victualled;
That is why I have arranged to bring music and song from the city.

THE PILOTMASTER

Bravo, friend postal inspector! I also have done my small part
To plan for our pleasure. When the first steamer approaches this evening,
He must be greeted with every signal this island can muster;
First we will fly the blue-yellow flag from the sloops and the lookouts,
Then from the pilot-knoll's peak our ancient cannon from Finland
Bought at a shore auction once for four riksdaler in bank notes
Thundering it shall announce our deliverer from the mainland
Our friend Kronander, captain first class and skipper on "Baggen."

The Children Sing Outside

We welcome you beloved sun,
Who chased away the north wind;
You have been sleeping since last year,
And rosy-cheeked awaken.

Warm up our earth, so rye will grow,
And fill the farmer's hayloft;
Warm sound and bay and wind and wave,
So we can go out swimming.

We welcome you beloved sun,
Shine over land and water;
Now songs ring out, the fiddles play,
We'll dance until the morning.

THE ESTATE CLERK

Hi! Do you see me? I have arrived, the first guest of the season,
I am Estate Clerk at the Magistrate's Court in Köping;
There I record the deceased's estate and am thus known in jest as
Death's godfather; remember me from last year? I am honored!
Thirty summers I've come here to saunter on Fagervik's beaches,
Taking my dip, and walking my round in the morning and evening;
Cheered by the cheerful as few, dispelling all thoughts about dying.
Gazing on sunshine and youth, I too become young in the spring time,
Like an old hollow oak that turns green but no longer can flower.
With my Lovisa I already have inspected my cabin;
Windows we opened to air the place out; we tidied and bustled;
Both dug the vegetable garden; I saw to the weeding and raking;
Parsley is there in its box, for without that powerful herb
The flounder and whitefish and perch, yes all fish requiring boiling
Taste like nothing at all; I know my beloved poor skerries.
We have sown dill, the wonderful dill, that's quite indispensable
When from the mainland in August the crayfish wiggling and plump
Are carried in spruce twigs out here, and from the outermost rocks

And islands the boats come to sell their tasty veal and their mutton,
Never forgetting, I hope, that the dill is completely essential,
He and none other is able to make boiled herring worth eating.
Radishes too I have sown, though more as a decoration,
They do so prettily garnish the buffet table each Sunday—
Flowers I planted as well, of well-known and popular species:
First I planted leukonium, in succulent, varying colors
Like a garland entwined by the bashful, sweet mignonette;
Nor did I leave out the asters, which cautious arrive in the autumn.
Plucky the aster stands tall in the frost when the others have wilted!
And when the last boat has left, and I move back into the city
I have one final bouquet to give to the steamship proprietress,
As a memento and thanks for all the heavenly moments
She has provided for me at the restaurant's sumptuous tables . . .
Oh! the exceptional eel, the salmon is aspic, dear fellows . . .

THE CUSTOMS COLLECTOR

Hang it, now Clerk, please stop, or you'll eat us to death with your fish tales,
And you'll be faced with the settling of all our estates before evening!

THE POSTMASTER

Well, Mister Clerk, like the earliest swallow in June you have come here,
Heralding springtime's arrival to us who live in the skerries
First bathing guest of the season, soon followed by so many others,
Bringing to our little town the jingling gold in our pouches;
Gold turns to silver and silver exchanged becomes glittering copper,
Rain on the pastor today tomorrow will pour on the sexton.
This way the village can prosper, the town pays its tax to the country.
Welcome to us, Mister Clerk, we all extend our greetings,
Share with us now our feast to honor the day, and the night too;
Here on this Trinity evening we drink to our health in the fountains,
Gold-yellow fountains that Mrs. Lundström has poured into bottles . . .
There I shall drink in your honor and wish that your life be a long one,
Not any shorter than ours, and longer yet by a measure.

THE ESTATE CLERK

Thank you, my friends, I most grateful accept your kind invitation,
First into line and last into bed will today be my motto
Bang! A shot just went off! And another! The steamer is coming!

At the fountain under oaks and birches stands a table set with bowls and glasses. At the table sit: the Estate Clerk, the Customs Collector, the Postmaster, the Poet, the Accountant, the Rector, and others.

THE ESTATE CLERK

Shouldering its yoke the sun gallops forth with glittering harness
Out of the zodiac Gemini, the fifth of its houses,
Leaves unreliable May and marches forth into Cancer.
Summer arrives in the North and the city-folk sweat in the city;
Schools finish up their semesters, the factories start their vacation.
Households prepare to depart, and the windows are chalked against sunlight,
Carpets are rolled to the wall and the winter clothes get an airing,
Everyone bustles about, the house smells of camphor and wormwood
Spread by the housewife herself to protect against moths and like vermin.
Then they are off; all hands to the pier where the steamer awaits!
Cast off and move out! Is nothing forgotten? We're off to the country!

Summer's first blush, this heavenly moment of youth and of beauty;
When the last hardy anemones in woodlands still linger
Until the cowslip emerges; she gives to the bees and voracious
Bumblebees honey and wax, to children she offers her garlands;
Inside the bounds of our garden parade the narcissi and tulips;
Newly dug beds of the velvety-blackest topsoil lie draped
In sweet-smelling snow from the flowering apple trees at the margins.
Tending his frames the gardener aerates, weeds, and waters—
Look at the board-straight lines of the crisp-white burgeoning lettuce,
And at the radishes' rows! They already rise from the surface
As if on rosy-red little feet they intend to escape us . . .
There stands the spinach in flocks, and the indispensable dill—
Be silent, my ravenous mouth!—I seem to be back where I started!

Midsummer, heavenly time, with its peonies and its lilacs!
Oh you sweet season of lilacs, lilacs but mostly the white ones
Whisper with fragrance as ever of youth of hope and of love,
They still remind me, yes still of a girl's glove scented with perfume
Or of a lace-bordered kerchief, a long ago winter ball trophy . . .

Then comes the day of the boats, with its rigging, splicing, and painting;
Fishing poles, pike lures, and hooks from the merchant have been
     requisitioned;
Cleared is our tennis court, soon multihued hats set to flapping,
Flashing in red, white, and blue, like giant blooms in the forest.
That time belongs to the young; the old must rejoice in their memory.

High summer day, when the wind stands still on the glittering water,
The sun he beats down on the shore and the children they bathe in the bay.
The cuckoo ceases its song when the scythe moves over the meadow.
Newly mown hay is raked and gathered on leaf-adorned wagons;
Milk and wild strawberries maybe a bowl of well-congealed filbunk[4]
Greet in the evening the sweaty, thirsting, hungering reapers.

Woman's Week comes in July,[5] a week that belongs to the ladies;
Name-day every day with port wine, coffee, and cookies—
Rose blooms arrive at their peak, but fall in force to the scissors:
Sara, Margreta, Johanna, Malena, Emma, Kristina,
All share the harvest of roses, the fairest deserving the fair.

The almanac promises rain; it rains fairly often, not always;
Nevertheless when it does, at the social club we all gather,
Choosing the board of directors and discussing the program.
Now we shall feast every night and play, and dance, and make merry,
Mostly we dance and eagerly, too, for the music is here now;
First class musicians on loan from the Royal Opera in Stockholm:
The first violin is quite good, but the second at one time was better,
Best is the double bass, and the clarinet is its equal,

But the piano, my friends, the piano is played like none other
By the director's wife, a student at the Conservatory,
She used to play for van Boom, I think it was in the 'sixties,
Since she has played for herself, and for her loved ones, no others.
Well! while inside the dancing continues in the grand ballroom
Then all the gentlemen, barring the youngest, of course, drink their liquor,
Or they go roll a few balls on the bowling-green on the hillside;
Down on the porch the ladies they sit in their parallel rows
Where, barring the youngest, of course, they brush off mosquitoes with
    branches;
Even mosquitoes belong to this joy, like the serpent in Eden,
Nasty mosquitoes, they sting as well-known and stop one from sleeping.
Sleeping? That's as it should be; in the light summer night in our north
We all should keep vigil, and shame on the person who sleeps before
    midnight—
Do instead as I do: take a lengthy nap after dinner.
Oh! You too heavenly night when in bed you finally tumble;
Mine a Gustavian bed[6] with a blanket of seabird feathers—
And let the night lamp burn for a lazy glance at the paper.
Briefly you battle the swarm of mosquitoes, that pesky procession,
Slip into dreaming, back to the winter's gloomiest evenings.
Senses grow heavy from thoughts as bleak as the autumn . . .
But when the lamp is extinguished there's daylight behind the drawn curtain,
Robins are already singing, the bay is splashing the shore line
North by northeast (half-east) the high summer sun has its purple
Spread in a glittering band which blinds like the bright borealis,
Peeks in my room! The new day begins! Then mosquitoes retire!
And with the sun, with the sun in your eye you finally slumber.

★

Drowsy the dog days drag by in the burning sign of the dog star;
All things stand parched and wilted, rotten, dusty, and sickly,
Heat compels us to sleep then flies bite us til we awaken,
Dahlias droop on their stalks and heavy the asters sink earthward— — —
Drought has cracked open the ground and the wells have run out of
    water . . .

Then from the east come rolling the thunderheads, blue-black and massive,
Lightning shoots off! A moment of silence! Then rumbling and rolling
Mangling and rangling![7] And so with a crash from the heavy artillery
Windowpanes shake from the clash and dampers clang in the chimney.
Torrents come plummeting down from the pitch-black clouds at the zenith,
Wind-gusts buffet so gruff, they bluster on the bay's billows,
People escape into sheds, they shut all the doors and the windows,
Birds creep away from the storm to the shelter of shivering birches,
Frightened the fishes sink down to the depths and dart into crannies . . .
Warrior jousting begins in the air, on the land, in the water;
Then all again settles down; like gunpowder smoke after battle
Clouds roll away, the sky becomes clear, all of nature turns silent,
Sunshine resumes once again to light us to warm us to burn us.
But despite heat and all else, the dog days contain pleasant moments—
Duck season opens, and berry picking begins with the cherries;
Field peas arrive at the market together with fresh-picked potatoes.
My! how the sugar dissolves when the fruits are preserved in the kitchens;
Fly paper you have to buy, but the family itself sews the fly net;
Children hold parties, the castor oil is sent out from the city;
Rumors of cholera spread predictable as the next sunrise;
Everyone keeps a strict diet; but the men insist on their cognac.

Then comes the time of the cutters, the Royal Sailing Society's,
And when the ringing cry flies about that the squadron has landed,
Quickly the parlor is swept, and the management gathers in meetings
Planning the ball they will give to the Naval Officers Corps . . .
The old men then say that's enough and to the Citadel sidle;
Drinking they prattle their nonsense, remembering how they were
    young once.
Now like a final ball of the summer August comes dancing
Late summer bears its fruit on the fallen flowers of spring;
The rye stands already in stooks and the wheat is yellowing slowly,
Erik he promised with spikes and Olof delivers the bounty[8]
Larsmass[9] arrives with its pears this year too, but none of them fancy;

Nevertheless the Astrakhan[10] windfalls appear on the walkways
Raspberry reaping continues, with melon and cucumber harvest;
Cucumbers they are my fruit, my favorite fruit, I confess it;
Better than others I grow them, then pack them in jars to preserve them,
Jars of a blue-green glass from a half-quart size to a gallon,
Bought from the Kosta Works, I think the store is by Monksbridge.
Hazelnuts seen on the bushes are now beginning to ripen
Nota bene we check if any are left from the summer;
Boys will eat them still green; the squirrels never refuse them.
Mushrooms start popping up like weeds after autumn showers—
Mushrooms taste best while they're fresh; they can also be salted, however—
Stop! We come round once again to August, to August in moonlight
Fireworks, lanterns, and flares are essential to the regatta—
Yes, my dear children—the old man he stumbles toward the finish—
Summer it draws to a close and evenings begin to grow darker;
Often the weather turns grey, people sit in their houses and shiver;
Anyone venturing out steps in dirt in mud and in water,
Spirits grow angry and heavy, regret begins before parting.
And fancy that, in old and in young a longing awakens
Longing for town, for the home, for the tavern and friends who are
        waiting . . .
Summer is over; we melancholy depart from the islands
As at a happier time from the islands and groves of the blessed . . .
Treuga Dei God's Peace, has drawn to a close in our nature
Feuding-rights start once again, with bickering, duties, and troubles:
All that is fair and is young is short like the Northern summer.

THE POET

Now I believe it is my turn to give you a speech at our banquet!
Thanks I will offer unasked to the clerk who sang about summer
And since the subject is free, I select—now listen dear fellows,
Love I select first of all, its heavenly joys and its sorrows.
Eros, the eldest of gods, yet humanity's youngest relation,
Eros the heavenly child who is born when man beholds woman,
Born by the lightning that lightning encountered from an eye flashing,

Born amid feuds that were finally closed in eternal embraces!
Eros my song! In minor and major keys, mostly minor.

Chrysaëtos[11]

What are those dreary crows seeking
Down there on the autumn heath?
At one time only the rooks
Sank down into naked trees.

What are those cranky crows seeking
That hundredfold circle out there?
    Is there carrion or feed
    On the butcher's cart?
    Or lies on the straw
    A dying beast
Or do the crows give a ball?

What are those cranky crows seeking
Down there in front of my house?
In lindens they hang,
And rock in the wind;
On night-branch they croak,
On morning-branch flap,
Awaiting the light of day.

What are those black dogs howling
Among the tobacco plants?
They stalk and snuffle in groves;
Keeping a careful watch.

What are those black dogs singing?
Are they singing over a corpse?
    They sit in their packs,
    And bellow and sing
    Necks stretched out,
    Ears pricked up . . .
    Noses hot and dry . . .
    You hear them growl,
When owls begin to shriek.

What are those yellow owls shrieking
On roofs of tobacco barns,
When the rusty and dented vane
Can barely stand up in the wind?
What is that rusty vane singing,
To the night-wind's sorrowful dirge?
    Is it a corpse?
    Maybe mine or yours?
    Is it sorrow or woe,
    Or a portent of death?
It is death, it is woe, it's a corpse!

What are those crooked men doing,
Down there on the snowy heath?
Perhaps setting snares for the hares
While the thaw still softens the soil.
    They carry the spruce-twigs,
    Cut down the stakes,
    Mark out the road[12]
    Measure their steps;
    A winter-road make,
    Will it hold or collapse
When it crosses the ice-covered lake?

What are those crooked men doing
At the entrance to my home?
The street gate creaks on its hinge
A snow blast hurtles it shut.
    Men spread out
    Branches in snow;
    Snowflakes fall
    Snow stars cold
    Fill up the tracks
    Crowding down
    All! All! All!
White and bitter as salt it falls!

Sleighs arrive, the drivers bellow,
Lanterns gasp, the day is snuffed.
Men are carrying, men are nailing . . .
Ended the tale! Ended the tale!

★

Then came a shriek . . .

★

Then came a shriek along the vaulted stair,
It travels over houses into alleys
And in the street the wand'rer quaked,
He clasped his hands as if in prayer.
Upstairs in an apartment of the empty house
A window opens, over naked treetops
A black-clad man leans out with lifted lamp,
He seems to want to light the heath below him;
And with a madman's voice he roars out like a beast
Just wounded in its narrow cage:

Chrysaëtos is dead!

The cry creeps over snowy heath, and weeps
Until it dies away against the northern hills,
The living forest then returns the cry,
And answers sobbing but succinct:

Chrysaëtos is dead!

★

In empty rooms alone he walks at random
And lights the lanterns, candelabras everywhere— — —
Upon the parlor wall the portrait
Regards him alien and cold— — —
He runs about from room to room and searches,
He seeks that which no more exists,
A hopeless search that agitates the madman,
And what he seeks no longer he recalls— — —
He opens drawers, cabinets, and side-boards— — —
From hall to kitchen next he steers his steps;
He searches under chairs and tables— — —
He stops when he has reached the vestibule.

There hangs a little coat forgotten
The collar's fur so gently worn
Where rounded cheek it used to fondle— — —
His memory revives, his eye burns red! . . .

And into the night . . .

And into the night on snow-covered heath
He rushes and searches,
He walks over ditches and over paths
While drift-snow billows about him!
Keep on! Keep on! Are those tracks?
In rain and in wind
He stumbles on stones
Is snared in the shrubs
The snowstorm stands like a wall . . .
Like a bull he charges the wind
He is blind, his cheek has turned pale,
Though his pulses race! Race wild!
Walk on your toes, or you will sink down,
And no one will see,
And no one will hear, if you pray, when you die!
When you're buried in snow-flowers' bed!
    Are you frightened my son?
    Look, heaven is black as a slate
    Without script, like a stone on a tomb
    But no one inside.
    Hold out! Persist or succumb!

       ★

He comes at last upon the southern hillocks,
Where tender birches mid the larch trees stand . . .
With bleeding heart he memories awakens— — —
Here with his arm around her waist he used to walk— — —

Far in the north—is it a fever vision
He faintly sees the empty house's grey facade
Like an express train standing in the station,
He sees his dwelling's windows in a lighted row!

And he shouts:

Is the train leaving soon?
Halloo!—Halloo!
It's a wedding train?
Did I glimpse the bride
My May-bride last year
In green and in white
In silk and a veil
In green and in white
Like the cherry in bloom
Out there by the wall?
I sat in the sun with sun in my soul . . .
That was then! . . . Chrysaëtos was mine!

★

And he sings:

Summer days with balmy breezes,
Azure waves, warm yellow earth,
Ivy creeps around the cottage,
Hangs above us as we dine.

On the long waves of the ocean,
We are swimming arm in arm,
Cooling ocean quenches fires
Sun ignited in our breast.

When you left the ocean's bosom
To your beauty I succumbed!
If I boasted, I'll be pardoned—
Nemesis cannot see you![13]

Chrysaëtos! . . .

Chrysaëtos, Gold-Erne, in your golden eye
One final time I saw the rising sun . . .
When we met above the clouds exalted

127

With my song I coaxed you down . . .
From your wing I then pulled out a quill pen
And with golden ink I wrote
Songs you know already—from Gehenna,
Which became our paradise!

★

     Summer evening . . .

    Summer evening, wind abated,
    From the beeches' verdant light,
    Eyes and cheeks aglow with sunshine— — —
    Homeward to our ivy house . . .

    Indian summer, silent forest,
    Even birds no longer sing,
    As the flower reaches ripeness,
    Down about you petals fall!

★

    Golden flax by iron fountain
    Silver linden, copper snake
       That's the Siren's riddle!
       It is yours and mine![14]

★

     While memories storm . . .

While memories storm like bare-winter's snow
He penetrates deeper into the forest.
The forest ends, he stands by a lake
Where furrows remain from the massive plow—
The winter road[15] lies there straight as a line
On each side bordered by stubbled spruces;
But over the road runs a streak of ink— — —
He stops discouraged and gazes.
Then in the darkness he hears a splashing, a pounding,
A panting a groaning a gurgling.
And then a howl, horrendous, without end.
Out of the darkness charges
A black and red colossus
Ice fields heave the water gushes.

Stooping spruces fight each other.
Ice floes are shattered like windows,
Shards chink together like glass,
Music from thousands of lutes
By an earthquake crushed to bits.
Now like a wounded whale,
The steamer passes, panting its coal smoke
Burying all in the gorge of its wake
And sea foam dances like pallid ghosts.

★

When the sun comes up . . .

When the sun comes up over ice field blue
The crooked men reappear to look
At the steamer's gaping path;
The crows along with the starlings come
To gather up this and that.
The dogs sit down on the rim of the ice
And howl as before in the groves,
Things went as they had foretold!

THE ACCOUNTANT

Now the turn is with me, but what poor man shall I sing of?
Sovereign Eros has spoken, the rest of us ought to keep silent;
Sorrow, his sorrow in teary meters our poet related.
Verse-war was not my idea, my fiddle was never a lyre;
Therefore a dream I wish to relate that I dreamed—at my desk.

I dreamed . . .

I dreamed I had become a cripple
And sat inside a room I think was mine . . .
Lit by the lamp's red glow I saw
A group of people whom I thought I knew.
I stared upon the lamp, but my left eye
A man at the piano saw . . .
He played, but not a single note I heard . . .
I only gazed upon the facial features
Of those who listened, how they changed . . .

In shady, shrieking harmonies . . .
But him who played I only could see from the back . . .
And how the shadow of his head kept moving
Around the sheets of music placed before him . . .
I also could make out the written notes:
From where I sat their crosses and their curves
Entwined themselves to look like facial features
Resembling in each point those of my guests . . .
The more he played, the larger grew the crowd
That kept collecting in that room
On tables, couches, chairs, and shelves!
The room turned stifling, and the door was opened,
First to the hall, and it was dark;
Then someone opens to the foyer;
And there the gas burned, white but faint,
And shone upon the floor squares, black and white,
Resembling an enormous chessboard.
Back there the staircase seashell twisted,
Its banister mahogany, right past
The narrow foyer window at the rear.
Upon the stair a tall and slender figure stood
Unmoving, black-clad, darkly veiled;
She leaned down as if bent by sorrow,
By meditation or profound despair . . .

My eye made keen by yearning for the new
Now penetrates behind the foyer window . . .
Outside the yard lies dark, but over it
Across the way I see a lit apartment . . .
Damask curtains, luxuries, fine furniture,
A dining room with splendidly set table
Prepared for only two but all was silver
The smaller items were of gold . . .
And lilacs, peonies in oriental vases,
The sideboard groaning under all good things
That sea and wood and garden can provide . . .
But I could see no person there . . .
My gaze which pushed its way inside became a thread
And by that thread I was dragged in

I, my entire person, I myself
And in an instant stood in the apartment!
I stopped, bedazzled, gazing in the dining room,
But frightened as if I had broken in . . .
I looked down on my paltry clothes
Down on my figure—and my crutches— — —
I thought I looked just like a wounded crow— — —
With dangling legs beneath the wing . . .
I wept with shame . . . A door flew open
And from the drawing room a woman stepped— — —
It was the woman from the stair . . .
But dressed now as a bride, she glowed with youth,
With beauty, goodness, childish self-delight . . .
She gave her hand to me, and with her gaze she said—
Now you are mine, and I am yours— — —
I sank down on my knees and in a moment felt
How wretched, truly wretched I appeared . . .
Unworthy to be loved by woman . . .
She smiled and asked me to stand up— — —
Just think, I rose and stood there young,
And hale, no more a cripple!
Have ever you cried out for joy, for bliss,
To feel your soul expand, grow larger
And send emotions forth of gratitude,
Forth endlessly, beyond the stars,
And farther yet, for there no boundaries exist . . .
Well, there I sat at table with my bride . . .
All matters gave me pleasure; words and thoughts
Together we begot and carried forth,
I found that I was full of sparkling wit,
Sometimes we rose up on the wings of thought
Sometimes we sought the depths, the matter's core;
Society and nature, dusky human fates
Deciphered as if reading from a book . . .
It was a wedding where two souls were joined— — —

I mentioned as you know that she was perfect
In manners, ways, not least of all in dress
But in that beauty I perceived a tasteless flaw

Which all the while had irked my eye . . .
A ribbon end hung loose, a red
Vexatious ribbon end on her right shoulder . . .
I kept my silence long, I struggled to say nothing,
But suddenly, while still we talked, my hand,
Refused to heed my orders, and I grasped
That ribbon end unthinking without malice . . .
But then, at once, my bride was changed,
A face as evil as the Gorgon's
Where every line became a little snake,
She showed me when the mask came off,
And with a voice a nightlife voice she hissed:
"So, you are one of those, a pedant
Who criticizes when you should admire?"
—"No," I replied, "but I desire your perfection,
And if I see a spot, I want to take it out."
And she: "You spot-remover, go away,
If I do not please you, I will find others!"
—"No doubt, just walk out on the street!
You will get many there, but never me."
And now began a word-war without end,
And neither understands just what the other wants;
A stormy row without intent without a goal
Unfolds itself and escalates to war . . .
It seemed to me we bickered days and weeks,
Yes, years went by, the candles melted down,
The sun arose and phases of the moon
Came one upon the other quick as seconds . . .
Sometimes I woke but instantly go back to sleep,
And like the argument the dream began again . . .
At last we battled, then bewailed
So bitterly our degradation— — —
Were reconciled, caressed, swore oaths of love,
And so we argued once again and battled— — —
I cried aloud: "Is there no end,
Is there no end to this damnation?"
There was no end; and every night the dream returns,
Which has become to me a second life!

THE RECTOR FROM SKÄGGA

Treading a trodden path I follow the worthy accountant,
Merely a student I am of our poetry's reverenced father,
Stiernhjielm[16] who first and who best has sung in an untainted Swedish,
In the hexameter's gait, the six-footed classical meter,
I will now sketch two miniatures of our Swedish landscape.

The Rye is Smoking

The rye is smoking in dawning air and on billowing ears,
The south-wind whispers so warm, little ripples float on the surface;
Flour-dust-like a veil hangs above it and wafts in the wind;
The nuptials of flowers it modestly hides just as Jupiter's clasp
Was hidden by clouds—and the yearly marvel occurs under cover.
Odors like oven-fresh bread are spread by the morning breezes;
Only a rustling, a shudder has passed through the whispering
    grass-blades;
Then all grows still; when the veil is raised up from the undulant meadow,
Secrets have secretly happened; the marvel is shown but in portents.
God's gift to us is our bread; inside the rye flower's bract-sheath
You can discover its use, it is called *Signatura rerum;*[17]
Cut by the artist's hand the sweetest daintiest models
Hang from the flowers forth and show us the tools of the baker.
Oven-rake, shovel, and notch, with the rolling pin, knife, and beater . . .
This I was taught by a child, I do not ask adults to believe me.
Lacking enclosure the pasture lies open to its surroundings,
Prey to the insects and creeping bugs, and to ravaging earth worms.
Who gave the crop its protection, who aids in the growth of the grass
    blade?
Weeds here reside for this purpose, expelling the damaging dross:
The bedstraw's narcotic odor, the chamomile's peppery smell
The cotula's putrid stench, the monkshood's poisonous vapor,
Even the daisy and cornflower, sought for midsummer's garlands
Hidden powers they have, for never the insects will touch them.

This indispensable grain thus by powerful herbs is protected
Just as our clothes are from moths by the bitter, the poisonous wormwood.
But when the rats and the mice, with the sweeping assemblage of sparrows
Come in their harrowing hoards to plunder the gardens and fields,
The corncrake soon scares them away with the rankling clink of his rattle;
Always unseen with his creak and his squeak, but everyone knows him
No one has seen him go off, and no one has seen him arriving,
Born to live flightless, he somehow moves south with the others in
    autumn.
Just how he travels, not even the learned have as yet discovered;
He leads his life unseen, disappears, then returns once again:
The corncrake is guardian of fields, he alone is gnome of the pasture.

★

The Meadow Barn

Walking one high-summer day between flowering meadows and pastures
Far from the gardens and houses, in search of those wood-paths less
    trodden;
Over a fence you stepped which crashes to pieces and frightens
Zig-zag-banded a snake which trickles back into a thorn-brake.
Quickly a shrike rises up, she sheckles, scoffs, and quackles.[18]
Now you follow the wood-fringe, by ferns and junipers bordered;
Closely cropped grass, an elf-ring with mushrooms, a single hay-flower;
Throw yourself onto a path with smoothly worn pine roots protruding,
Glittering needles fragrant with resin, a peril for walkers;
Ants have constructed a hill at the foot of a pine like a coal-stack;
Dark as the myrtle the blueberry thicket stands. The white Pyrola
Twines itself in them like orange blooms in the crown of the bride.—
The woodpecker pecks at his hole, and the siskin up in the tree tops
Nests in the swaying branch of a pine straight and high as a mast;
The wood-dove cries out its pain as a woman cries out in child-birth.
Mighty the forest and dark when it broods on solemnities sacred.
Looks like the room of a thinker with curtains heavy and green
Inviting the spirit to work, to labor of thought and to worship.
Look, it grows lighter again, a clearing opens before you;

Stoutly the stumps remain; by the roots wild strawberries flourish,
And in the moss-bed protected stands the tender Linnaea,
Peach-red the delicate bells with a fragrance of milk and of almond
Elegant as a batiste pin fastened in green-glowing velvet;
Straight as a straw stands the stalk, so dainty, so graceful, so fancy.
Into the spruce-wood twilight the path once again meanders,
Blacker the tree trunks stand; a wood-tarn lies in a hollow,
Lilies as white as wadding rise out of the sludgy water;
Nuptials they hold up here in the light, in the sun, in the open,
Then they dive down to the bottom, to hide their pain in the lake slime.
Short and sweet is the season of love throughout all of nature
Starts out so heavenly high and ends in the depths of the swamp.

The winding way suddenly stops, like a glittering sea lies the meadow;
Flowering clover lea, with honey and raspberry fragrance,
Bees and bumblebees diligent court the red and white trefoils;
The meadow he sings! Stand silent and hear the chorus of singers;
Does it not seem when you hark as if flowers themselves were the singers?
Blossom-song, blossom-scent blend with the breeze in melodious union,
Graspable only by him who has freed himself from a marriage
Poisoned by vanity and been born once again into nature.

Now you follow a ditch, a skylark nests by the ditch-bank;
Here the clover field ends, and the meadowland runs to the pasture;
Smooth as a floor the delightful meadow with oak and with aspen,
Much like a courtyard, protection it finds from the spring pasture's fencing.
Lonely a house now appears, a grey one, resembling a temple;
The vestibule holds up the lofty roof made of timber turned hoary;
Windows are not to be found; here dwell neither creatures nor
   humans— — —
It stands alone by itself, the symbol of perfect aloneness,
This is where you would live, if alone you could ever be happy,
Without yourself, I mean, but alone you are never alone;
Your ego follows you round like the shadow follows its master.
This is the meadow barn, home of dried hay, the mansion of flowers;

One true companion she has, the massive moss-covered linden,
Linden bewitching tree, in nature she shuns all society;
Only in park avenues is she forced to stand pruned and paraded;
High as the dome of a church she forms for the temple a tower,
And among trees she bears the loveliest leaves, little heart shapes,
Hearts that chime in the wind, and the flower suffused with a halo
Borne through the air on two wings when the fruit falls to earth fully
   ripened.
Meadow barn, mansion of flowers, with fragrance of spring-sprouts and
   clover,
Under her eaves she allows but a single swallow's nest shelter.
One solitary pair has withdrawn here away from life's throng;
Devoted, they nourish their young ones, leaving the world to its troubles.
They are the meadow barn's guests, in her house she suffers no others.

THE POSTMASTER

Well, so the turn is with me now, and pitiful how shall I manage?
I was not born very bright, I cautiously crawl on earth's surface,
True, I once climbed as high as up to the roof of a barn,
Heard there the weather vane's song, it was rusty just like the old man,
The old man who sits here with you while muttering, tippling, and babbling.
Now then, without more excuses— — —I do not have any pretensions.

The Vane Sings[19]

There sits a vane on the roof of the barn,
Tobacco barn— — —
He only sings straight to the point
In northern wind— — —

In frost,
A rust-
y shape;
Scrape;
Scrape;
It is a dragon

On a spire;
Sharpened teeth;
Turning wind.
Vip;
Rip;
Wip;
Weep.
Strip,
The leaves.
How's that?
Tobacco leaves.

Ind;
Grind;
Snuff,
Packet;
Packets
Pleases
The teacher.
Guardsmen;
Liquor,
Bicker
Knives
At the ball!
Corporal!!!

The master,
Tobacco master
Lurking,
fur, fur, fur,
Furious,
Pimply;
ink ink ink
Chink;

Chinkspur;
Slap,
Drunk,
Sheer chance,
Crisis— — —
Police!!!

★

There sits a vane on the roof of the barn,
Tobacco barn
At times he displays better taste,
In southerly wind.

Autumn,
Comfort!
Comfort me!
Don't strut
About!
Iron broken,
Candles snuffed.
You hope —
Are snubbed.[20]
The dragon
On the spire
Whistles
Gnashes
Teeth;
Bends . .
Wobble
Sprain —
Ock ock ock,
Lock —
Locked?
Worsen
Toil, toil, toil.

Yet a while.

Left Right

Rusty Stiff

North and South

Sorrow Death

Weep,

Weep.

THE CUSTOMS COLLECTOR

The worst has been left until last, the jester clatters his rattle,
For the child who was weeping. Laughing makes one live longer.
Here is my birdsong, then, which I heard in my childhood in Skåne.[21]
There my cradle has stood, and the song I once learned from my nanny.

The Nightingale's Song

Ih,ih,ih,ih,ih! Was it we? It was we!

We it was! Quoy, oy, oy, oy, oy, oy!

Look, my lovely, lull-lull-lull-lull—Was it we?

Ihih! Look! my lovely! It swerves, arrrrrrrrrr-itz!

Lull-lull-lull-lull-lull-lull! Was it they? See!

See you, see you, see you, see you?

Nanny!—Nanny! Shut, shut, shut, shut—see you, see you?

Nipple; nipp, ipp, ipp, ipp, ipp, ipp!

White, white, white, white, white, white, see my wee one!

Tut, tut, tut, tut, tut, tut, sat'n, sat'n, sat'n, see!

Weep, weep, weep, weep, weep, weep, eeh!

So, so, so, no, no, no, say, say, say, say now!

Ji, jih, goh, goh, goh, goh, god-help, nanny aitsch!

THE POET

Feasting is over, our Trinity Night has merrily ended;
Now the church-year calendar's holiday-free time commences,
This part shall last until Christmas; but that seems to me an illusion:
Summer itself is a feast, a months-long holiday feasting.

Rest from our work and our struggles, we worship out in the open;
Sunday-peace reigns in our spirits, the special rejoicing of Sundays
We can enjoy every day, as many as the week offers.
Night has departed, and Saturday night is now yesterday;
The spring sun again has been lit, and sabbath bells ring in the distance;
Let them proclaim our feast days, our summer, our peaceful existence!
Though we part now, we will meet soon again, we fraternize daily.
Therefore we say not good night! We wish each other good morning!

By the Outermost Cape

1

By the outermost cape on a whitened crag
A house stretches upward grey and decaying;
The doors stand open one windy night;
Inside in the hall someone plays the piano.

An unknown sailor is tacking out on the bay,
Alone at the helm, with the sheets at the ready;
He hears in the sail, when he tacks through the wind
A bar played on the piano, one only.

Then all is still; but he raises his hat
And sends back to her a thanks on the breezes,
And she in the house, she captures it—
It was like a kiss on the cheek from a stranger.

One wonderful moment they then embraced;
They gave and they took enveloped in darkness;
They never once heard each other from that moment on—
Or until they died ever saw each other.

2

It is night and calm since the sun went down,
In dusk on the point a tree grove sleeps by the fish-rail,
Daylight birds have vanished from sight,
The waves lie resting under their sea-green blanket.—

The doors to the hall then are opened wide,
Released they leap in the air the sounds once fettered:
The piano sings, and the swell of the notes
Awakens the night, asleep in its rosy vestments.—

A ripple now cracks the ocean's mirror,
The trees are sighing as if they were sails,
A boat, a white one glides silently forward,
Two, many, hugging the shore;
Light-clad folk in the stems of their rowboats
They listen with reverence, oar in hand.— —

Then birds awaken on islets and skerries!
On snowy wings the seagulls come gliding,
Silently searching, from far and near;
They alight on the water which rocks in delicate circles.
The wagtails they stand on the stones in the shoreline;
Pasture sparrows arrive from the headlands,
Magpies from forests and crows out of fallows,
Mute, bewildered at first, they soon settle down.

Out of the depths a phalanx of fishes shoots upward,
Bleaks dart about and pikes slap their tails on the surface,
Down by the pier the glittering shiners and roaches
Wont to hear naught but the whirring mosquito,
Stop with gaping mouths in their schools to hear
Rest on their fins afraid to disturb.

Night-moths dance in a sonorous ring to the music,
Alders curtsy and reeds bow their heads in the cove;
All of nature has wakened and listens;
The rock face gleams like a moistened eye
Teary with dew caressing the stones;
The mountain weeps at the music's kiss.—

In the blue-white vase of the summer sky
A star is fastened, starwort-like, one only,
And in his final phase the lunar globe
He waits to light the lamp of autumn—

Then on the shore a surge of wave on wave
Is heard as the piano's tones grow silent;
The wake left by a steamer no one saw,
An echo maybe from another region.— —

The birds arise and skittish fly away,
The fishes mute return down to the bottom,
And all grows still, one single evening cloud
Sinks down and covers up the moon's red disk.

3

Who walks in the hall tonight, in the night?
On whimpering floorboard, on shrieking nail,
And peers out over the blackened bay?—
Where treads your foot, you pallid corpse,
Your little foot, so light, so sweet?— —
So young, so much, so hard
Your heel it once trod on hearts,

Oh!

Why sit alone in the hall in the dark
And play the piano with trembling hand,
Shaking the house on the windy rock?
You lady white on a lonely shore?—
Out of the black piano grave
Your sad self rises up.—
Your sadness brings joy to others, though,

Though!

The Dutchman

The First Song

The seventh year without destination I sailed
The ocean desert, and fled the shores' temptations
A Christmas light glimmered at times, at times a midsummer's pyre
From unknown lands in the distance beckoned.

And never a flower I saw there, never a tree
No yellowing field, no verdant meadows;
But when I gazed down into darkling depths
In miles-long beds there floated the algae.

Down there lay my summer, my consolation;
I saw by the sun when the equinox line signaled springtime.
The movable stars proclaimed when autumn began;
The pain in my scars announced to me winter's arrival.

The seventh year—for such were the terms of my fate—
I aimed the bow at the nearest shoreline,
The ban that was hurled from Rome itself,
It sent my ship with its crew into a safe harbor.

One night I alit on the coast; came into a town,
And in the cathedral square I met a pilgrim;
He spoke to me—I remember his words—
Beneath the Madonna by the great portal.

"My son," he spoke, "the time of torment is nigh;
A seventh time you near your trial's terrors
The sweetest the fairest that earth has to give
Once more shall tear your heart into bloody tatters.

What good hesitation? Powers have thus ordained;
You spat at the sea and clenched your fist toward heaven,
Now you must pay for your pride, and hundred-fold—
As Omphale's[1] slave you must sit at your weaving."

He gave me his hand, and down by Mary's Spring
He brought me beneath a house in a narrow alley—
There stood a woman— — —In short, my flame was lit—
Before I could rear, my monk had vanished.

The Second Song

What is it? Who is it?
A human being in white veils,
A chorus of lines' harmonies
Beneath the veil revealed.
A universe made small,
An image of the Mighty Cosmos!
Behold the thigh's immense parabola, arced like the comet's path,
Which leads out into spaces guessed at, but not known . . . .
She turns around, and soon I see
The same lines changed to half-ellipses,
Which form the earth's course round the sun,
When joined they shape the egg,
And from the womb, its focal point, the radii leap out.—
Down from the shoulders to the groin is traced
The holy hexagram,
Resembling glorious Orion on the starry vault,
The navel demarcating there the Belt . . .
Through which the sky's equator runs its course,
And at the bottom rests upon the spheric triangle
Formed by three convex arches:
A flattened cupola upon the temple's roof,
The temple wherein Motherhood is worshipped!

Above the torso with a myriad of tiny curves
From solar crown and from the lunar crescents;
The breast's two hemispheres are earth.
Look at the kneecap's cloud-spot borrowed from the Milky Way
And at the slender bowing calf
Curved like a body thrown through space!
The foot's arch and the shoulder's rounding
Yes, and the swelled curves of the arm,
All move out from the sphere:
A symphony of spheral harmony;
Out from the sphere and from the cone,
The light cone sent out from the sun itself!

So were you, Woman, shaped by light from heaven
A shape formed in the Shaper's image,
Of pieces borrowed from the Universe.
And therefore you are All!
All-giver,
Without whom I am strictly nothing!
But child of heaven! From the earth,
From all of nature's kingdoms fashioned was
The fine form where your spirit was to dwell.
Your ear received from shell and clam its shape;
Your mouth is like a flower with its honey pockets,
Its essence though a stoma through which plants take breath.
The curved line of your nose's wings
One finds in grapes' and melons' tendrils.
Your pearly teeth were by the fish-scale given form.
Your eye a precious stone, as black as onyx, sapphire-blue,
Sometimes it also can be agate-brown.
The pupil fitted in its shell
The blue-white egg shell of a dove,
Which rests within a bed so sweetly bordered by

The black web from a heron's feather—
To what shall I compare your hair?
A wild horse mane, no to the purple mollusk's silky threads,
No, to the blue sea's finest algae,
The meadow's grandest grass, the germ, the fescue,
And most of all the Pampas grass's heavy plumes!
Perhaps the silk worm spun it into linen sheeting
To hatch the butterflies?
Or has the spider spooled this magic thread
To catch its golden flies?
When Uranus in first earth dug
And Gaia, Mother Earth, sat spinning
That, Eve, became your locks,
The first bride's veil,
The infant's swaddling clothes!
With them you dried your tears
With them you hid your nakedness,
When out of paradise you walked
Upon earth's thorny path.
Within the shadow of that healthy forest
You rest your weary eyes,
When from your hand the needle drops at night,
When all your strength the sickly child has sapped
And sucked the last drops of white blood
Out of the alabaster bowls, your breasts!

*

Alas, I too have rested in the shade of locks
In mother's lap and at wife's bosom once—
They were so light, as delicate
As tender shoots upon a birch in spring;
Once, they were black as cypress;
A scourge of braided snakes
They struck my eye;

And wove themselves into a hair shirt
Which I was forced to carry while I starved!
Oh loving scourge . . . .

The Third Song

We stand once again next to the cathedral
My pilgrim and I.
One year has passed, a ghastly, unforgettable—
And all is finished.
My ship in the harbor tugs at its anchor
It longs for the sea as do I.—
That I still live is a miracle
And a heaven's grace,
But just the same . . .
My hair is white now
My eyes drained of their color.—
Is there a name for all the agonies I suffered?
The calculated cruelty,
The conscious lies,
The skillful slander,
Groundless and irrational
As hate itself!
And just the same . . .
I went to wedding joy
As to a children's feast;
I put my fate into her hands,
I laid my head into her lap
As in a friend's,
Omphale! Omphale!
Then I awakened from my lover's sleep
And found myself held captive
By my worst enemy.
Deep in a stinking well,
Chained to a corpse,

Which caused my soul to rot
Piece by piece.
Where did you find the power, little worm,
To thus torment the Strong?
From me and from my manly strength
You got it!
I gave, and you received;
But when I turned it off
And took back what was mine
Then your omnipotence was finished.
There was no vice, no crime
No sin no baseness,
No wrong, no evil
That I did not endure . . .
And just the same . . . — —
Now that I'm free again
And as the moment of departure nears,
I see again the enemy as friend;
A genial joking with the past ensues . . .
I realize the past was but a trial!
And that I did not die down in the snake pit
A victim to those torments
It makes me truly glad and almost disappointed,
But mostly grateful and inclined to reconcile;
In short: in spite of all, and just the same—in life
One usually ends up in a vise
For nothing we get nothing back
And never victory without deep scars . . .
Farewell then, Omphale, my former mistress,
Now I can laugh in secret at your arts;
I was a slave, but so were you;
I am a man again, but you are just a little evil woman!

The Wolves Are Howling

The wolves are howling at Skansen,
Ice floes bellow at sea,
Spruces crack on the hillside,
Weighted by early snow.

The wolves are howling in winter,
Dogs reply from the town;
The sun went down after dinner,
Night begins in the day.

The wolves are howling in darkness,
Street lamps light up the sky
Shine like the borealis
Over the houses in rows.

The wolves are howling in wolf-pits,
Now they have tasted blood,
Long for the fjells and forests,
When they see northern lights.

The wolves are howling above us,
Howling with hatred hoarse,
People traded their freedom for
Prisons and celibacy.

★

Stillness reigns, the wind subsides, the city's tower clock strikes twelve;
Silent sleds glide on the snow as if on newly polished floors.
Dogs no longer bark on streets, the final tram has made its rounds,
Lights go out, the city sleeps, not a branch moves on the trees;
Black as velvet vaults the night sky reaching up to endless depths
High Orion swings his sword, the Plough has stood itself on end.

Fires in the grate have died, now only distant smoke remains;
From a chimney obelisque it rises as if from a giant's hearth
It's the baker, who at night prepares for us our daily bread— — —
Blue-white, straight up sails the smoke; but look—just now it turns to red.
It's a fire!
It's a fire! It's a fire! It's a fire!

And a red-flaming globe rises up like a moon at its fullest;
And the fiery red turns to white then to yellow and bursts like a sun-
 flower's perianth.
Is it maybe the sun rising out of black clouds from the ocean of houses?
Where each roof is the crest of a wave, which is dark as the grave.
Now the sky stands aflame, every tower and dome in the town,
Every spire and staff, every alley and nook, lit up as if it were day!
Every cable and wire of copper turns red like the lowest tuned strings
 of a harp,
On the house fronts each pane glows with flames, and the snow-covered
 chimneys are shining like beacons.
Neither sun nor moon is the cause of this light! Nor a feast conflagration!
It's a fire! It's a fire! It's a fire!
*

But now up on the mountain so recently covered by night, there is light
 there is life.
From the wolf-pit there rises a howling as if they were stabbed through
 with knives,
Of hatred, revenge; it's the passion of arsons, a murderer's joy—
Then of laughter a bark from the fox-hole escapes, they are glad, they are
 fierce, they are pleased.
And the bears in their cage, they dance on their heels with a grunting like
 new-slaughtered swine
But the lynx in its burrow sits silent, you see but the teeth of a glittering
 grin.
*

And the seals are shouting their woe! Woe over the city!
Shouts as from drowning men at sea.
And all the dogs howl in chorus;
Yelp, bellow, and bark,
Tug at their chains, their chains,
Singing, crying, and whining
Like the souls of the damned!
They have compassion, only they, the dogs,
For their human friends
What sympathy!

Now the moose awaken, princes of Northern forests,
They gather and order their spindly legs,
Come to a trot in a controlled volte
Inside the fence's pen,
Lurch into fence posts
Like sparrows into windows;
They low perplexed,
Wondering if day has come again.—
A new day, like all the others,
Just as tortuously long
Without any apparent motive
Than to be followed by night.— — —

Next the bird world startles awake:
Eagles shriek and flap,
Tempting tired wings,
Try in vain a soaring flight,
Butt their heads on iron posts,
Bite the bars, claw, cling,
Until they sink to earth,
and lie there lame,
With dragging wings as if on their knees—
On bended knees, praying,

For a mercy blow
To return them to the air
And freedom.

The falcons whistle and dash
Like feathered arrows—here and there;
The buzzards lament,
Like ailing children— — —
The tamed wild geese awaken
And strike up with taut throats
A chord of cowherd horns.—
The swans swim silent
Snapping between ice floes
At the mirrored flames
Darting about like goldfish
On the pond's surface.
Standing still they stick their heads
Into the black water—
The white swans—
Bite themselves fast to the bottom
To escape seeing
Heaven burning up.

*

The dark prevails again, the siren
To town and country has proclaimed new peace;
A smoke cloud stretches out across the skyline
The picture of a black enormous hand.

Notes

Notes

From *Poems in Verse and Prose*

"In Nyström's Studio"

1. This park is behind the Royal Library, where Strindberg later worked as an assistant librarian.

2. A bed-bench is a common item of furniture in Swedish country kitchens: a deep, hollow bench with a lid that opens up to reveal a bed.

3. *Det skönas värld* (1879), by the Norwegian Lorentz Dietrichson (1834–1917), was a presentation of aesthetics based on the teachings of Hegel's student Friedrich Theodor Vischer. (Göran Söderström, *Strindberg och bildkonsten* [Uddevalla: Bohusläningens AB, 1972], 14). Lorentz Dietrichson formed *Namnlösa Sällskapet* (the Nameless Society), also known as the Signatures, in Uppsala in 1860.

4. Carl Michael Bellman (1740–1795) was an author of humorous and lyrical verse; the most famous are *Fredman's Epistles* and *Fredman's Songs*. He is considered one of the greatest figures in Swedish literature. Strindberg disapproved of Bellman on moral grounds in his early youth, found him acceptable in his middle years, and again rejected him later in life. Strindberg excluded "In Nyström's Studio" from the 1911 edition, possibly, in part, because he feared Bellman's mystical influence over him since he had once impersonated Bellman by posing for Nyström's statue.

5. An island in Stockholm on which the open-air museum Skansen (see "The Wolves Are Howling") and the Nordic Museum are located. Because of its large parklands, it is a piece of the country within the city limits. Bellman writes often of picnics and excursions to Djurgården, an event with which any Stockholm resident would be familiar.

"Indian Summer"

1. Heinrich Heine (1797–1856) was a German lyrical poet and literary critic. Most important to Strindberg, especially during the mid-1870s, were Heine's satirical poems adopting a world-weary pose and specializing in nonce compound adjectives.

From "Exile"

"Exile" describes a voyage Strindberg took in October of 1876 from Stockholm to Kristiania (now Oslo), Norway, and then across the North Sea to Paris. In spite of the date in the title, most of the poem was probably written in 1882 or 1883. See note 9 in the introduction for problems with dating "Exile." The poem contains seven sections, all but the first and fourth in free verse in the style of Heine. Strindberg offers satirical observations about Norwegian, English, and French culture, ending with an admission of homesickness, as he will do again in *Sleepwalking Nights*.

1. Jacob Church is a seventeenth-century church across from the Royal Opera House.

2. A form of arrack, this sweet liquor is distilled from the coconut palm or a mash of rice and molasses.

3. Strindberg voices his objections to his contemporaries in these two stanzas, criticizing what he considers to be the amateurish writings of his colleagues and the Swedish tendency to glorify anything French. Strindberg had, since the 1870s, been a vocal proponent of indigenous influences on Swedish contemporary art.

4. This line refers to the 1810 election of Jean Baptiste Jules Bernadotte (1763?–1844), a general under Napoleon, to be the heir to the Swedish throne. Sweden had endured a troubled period, during which it had lost much of the land it had conquered in the seventeenth and eighteenth centuries, and was feeling threatened on all sides by Russia, Prussia, Germany, and England. The royal line had died out, and many felt that Sweden needed a leader well versed in foreign affairs and military tactics. They therefore turned to Bernadotte. He was crown prince and regent from 1810 to 1818, then succeeded Karl XIII to become Karl XIV Johan, king of Sweden and Norway. He ruled until his death in 1844. The current Swedish king is his descendant.

5. Gotthold Ephraim Lessing (1729–1781) is a German dramatist and critic. Dressers in the baroque style had protruding bellies.

6. Nikolaus is probably Tsar Nikolaus I (1796–1855) of Russia. Olof Ulrik Torsslow (1801–1881) is a Swedish actor. Emelie Högqvist (1812–1846) is a Swedish actress and mistress to King Oscar I, with whom she had two sons.

7. Frans Michael Franzén (1772–1847) is a Finland-Swedish bishop and poet. Johan Olof Wallin (1779–1839) is a Swedish archbishop, poet, orator, and hymn writer. Wilhelm August von Braun (1779–1839) is a Swedish poet and novelist. He specialized in humorous, somewhat risqué poems. Therefore, he is the "faun" among the "seraphs."

"Loki's Curses"

1. Son of Loki and Angurboda, the monstrous Midgard serpent encircles the earth. His writhing causes tempests. At *Ragnarök*, the end of the world, perhaps better known to English-speaking audiences as *Götterdämmerung*, the Midgard serpent, also known as Jörmungandr, together with his siblings the Fenris Wolf and Hel (see "The City Journey," note 8), will increase in strength by feeding on human evil until they

break their bonds. The serpent will be killed by Thor, the god of thunder, who in turn will be drowned by the sea of venom issuing from the dying serpent's jaws.

2. Volhynia or Volyn is a wooded area of northwestern Ukraine. It was originally independent, became part of Lithuania in the fourteenth century, was ceded to Poland in 1569, and remained a Polish territory until 1793 when it again became part of the Ukraine. Because of Swedish interests in the region in the sixteenth, seventeenth, and eighteenth centuries, various battles were fought there by Swedish armies.

3. Here, Strindberg alludes to the Paris Commune, the 1792 revolutionary government, headed by Danton, Robespierre, and Marat, which fell in 1794, and to the Commune of 1871, modeled on the first Commune, led by socialists and anarchists, allied to the Internationale. Both were characterized by bloody battles.

4. At the end of the world, once all the gods have killed each other, fire will heat the oceans until they boil and consume the lands. Loki is also known as the god of fire.

"The Boulevard System"

The poem was probably written in February 1883, when the clearing for the Karlaplan fountain and adjoining boulevard was begun. See Olof Lagercrantz, "Strindbergs satiriska och polemiska diktning mellan Röda rummet och utresan 1883" (Unpublished monograph, Stockholm University Library), 2. The poem quickly became popular with members of Young Sweden and others who fancied themselves nihilists; they saw in the poem metaphorical arguments for anarchy and nihilism. Although they doubtless read Strindberg's message correctly, it is a somewhat ironic one, since the poem depicts the renovation of one of Stockholm's wealthiest and most exclusive neighborhoods

"The Epicure"

1. Slussen, the Stockholm Locks, is located at the southern juncture of Lake Mälar and the Baltic.

"For the Freedom of Thought (November 6, 1882)"

1. November 6, 1882 was the 250th anniversary of the death of Swedish King Gustaf Adolf (he is often known to English speakers as Gustavus Adolphus) at the Battle of Lützen, November 6, 1632, a major battle in the Thirty Years War.

2. This line alludes to a line in a Swedish hymn, *Förfäras ej du lilla hop* ("Do not be frightened, little group"), officially Gustav Adolf's "Field-Hymn," written in 1631 by his chaplain Jacobus Fabricius. The king's troops often sang it before battle, including the day of November 6, 1632, when the king was mortally wounded at the Battle of Lützen. I am indebted to Professor George Schoolfield of Yale University for information about the hymn.

3. Magdeburg was destroyed in 1631, in one of the bloodiest battles of the Thirty Years War. Of the 36,000 inhabitants, 30,000 were killed.

4. Monk is the liqueur Benedictine.

5. This is an allusion to Strindberg's *Det nya riket: Skildringar från attentatens och jubelfesternas tidevarv* (The New Kingdom: Stories from the Age of Assassination Attempts and Jubilees), published in 1882, a major impetus for his departure from Sweden the following year and for the creation of *Poems in Verse and Prose*. This part of the poem may also allude to the historian Julius Mankell, who had published a revisionist history of Gustav Adolf. (Martin Lamm, *August Strindberg*, vol. 1 [Stockholm: Albert Bonniers Förlag, 1940], 195). Strindberg would have viewed such a venture sympathetically.

From *Sleepwalking Nights on Awake Days*

"The Third Night"

1. Denis Papin (1647–1712) was a French physicist, who lived mostly in England. He made improvements in the air pump and invented the condensing pump and the safety valve; he is credited with being the first to use steam to raise a piston.

2. Although Strindberg's shifts in tense are erratic, the shift to the simple past from the conditional suggests that Strindberg is remembering the times he walked in Humlegården Park next to the Royal Library, where he worked before leaving Sweden in 1883.

3. This is probably an allusion to Omar I (581?–644), second orthodox caliph (634–644). He initially opposed the prophet Mohammed, then later converted to Islam. He extended the Moslem empire, defeating the Persians and conquering Syria, Palestine, and Egypt. He was assassinated at Medina by a Persian slave.

"The Awakening"

1. Septennate refers to the seven-year term of a French president.

2. Concordat may refer to the concord between Sweden and Russia on December 23, 1882, or to the Concordat of Worms of 1122.

3. The nets are the snares that priests, like spiders, lay for their prey; perhaps, more specifically, this is a reference to the Jesuit Order.

4. The friend has joined the International Order of Goodtemplars; he has stopped drinking alcohol.

5. In 1889, Strindberg was still infuriated by a parody of *Det nya riket* (The New Kingdom) by Wilhelm Bergstrand, who, under the pseudonym Michel Perrin, in December, 1882, wrote "The Newest Kingdom. Characteristic Tales from the Age of Thoughtlessness and Insolence. I: The Realist." Michel is the Swedish equivalent of Reynard; hence Strindberg's use of fox metaphors, which he also used frequently in his satirical poems in *Poems in Verse and Prose*. Strindberg likely was also thinking about The Song of Solomon 2:15: "Take us the foxes, the little foxes, that spoil the vines: for our vines have tender grapes."

6. This is probably a reference to Bismarck's famous statement: "The great problems of our age will be solved not by debate and vote but by blood and iron." The section illustrates Strindberg's perception that Sweden has become Germany's tool and has betrayed her own people and her neighbors.

7. Bonzes are Buddhist priests. Strindberg, however, may be referring only to Christian ministers, and, perhaps, also to Young Sweden, a group of young writers by whom Strindberg felt betrayed. They saw him as one of their heroes in their early years but did not, in Strindberg's opinion, rise to his defense when his critics mocked him.

8. Here Strindberg probably compares Stockholm's corruption to the devastating eruption of the Indonesian volcano Krakatoa in 1883 and to the destruction of Pompeii by an eruption of Mt. Vesuvius in 79 A.D.

9. The excavation of Pompeii is likened to the rebuilding of Stockholm. Although Pompeii has been excavated, it is still dead.

10. These lines may refer to the 1810 treaty between Sweden and Russia. After Russia's march north to the Gulf of Bothnia and southward to Umeå, Sweden was forced to capitulate and give up all of Finland, Åland, and part of Swedish Lappland. The poem lists the ways in which Sweden has betrayed others, especially Denmark, Finland, and Strindberg, because of cowardice.

11. Denmark lost two battles to the Germans at Dybböl, in 1848 and 1864. Als fell in 1864. Many Swedes felt that Sweden should have assisted Denmark in the battle, but it did not.

From *Word Play and Minor Art*

In the 1902 edition of *Fagervik och Skamsund* (Fair Haven and Foul Strand), "Holy Trinity Night" appeared as a separate work and "Street Pictures," "The City Journey," "Cloud Pictures," and "The Dutchman" appeared under the title *Ordalek och småkonst* (Word Play and Minor Art). In the 1905 edition, of the poems included here, were added "By the Outermost Cape" and "The Wolves are Howling." In this edition, "Holy Trinity Night" was enfolded into *Word Play and Minor Art*.

"Street Pictures"

All the scenes described Strindberg could see from his apartment on Banérgatan, where he moved after his marriage to Harriet Bosse failed. In the poem's second part, he sees Nybroviken, a Lake Mälar bay, Skeppsholmen, a small wooded island in Stockholm, and Katarina Church, topped by a round cupola, a globe, and a cross. See Gunnar Ollén, *Strindbergs nittonhundratalslyrik* (Stockholm, A. B. Seelig & Co., 1941), 277–78. Stockholm's first power station was completed in 1892 at Regeringsgatan 32 and was known as Brunkebergsverket. This might be the inspiration for the dynamo in the poem's third part.

1. It was the custom in Stockholm, as in many European cities, for merchants to advertise their shops by hanging pictures of their products on signs outside.

2. The Norns are the three Fates of Norse mythology. Traditionally, they often do good deeds.

"Cloud Pictures"

1. In the Swedish original, Strindberg uses the verb *betäcka*. As in English, *betäcka* ("to cover") can also mean "to impregnate."

2. The poem was written during a time of reconciliation for Strindberg, when differences with relatives, including the children from his first marriage, were temporarily forgotten.

"The City Journey"

The prototype of the organist was probably the Årdala organist F. A. Walin, with whom Strindberg lived in the summers of 1857–1859 (as noted by the editors in *Letters* VII, 89). The organist in "The City Journey" lives in a settlement on the westernmost banks of Lake Mälar, west of Stockholm. When the first version of "The City Journey" appeared in 1902, some critics faulted the hexameter for being too irregular. Strindberg uncharacteristically reworked many lines for the 1905 version. This was the version used in the Landquist standard edition (1912–1920), although later many critics expressed a preference for the first version, arguing that its greater terseness made for better poetry; others have suggested that the two versions be combined by an editor to arrive at a third, ideal version. The volume containing *Word Play and Minor Art* in the new National Edition (Gunnar Ollén, ed., vol. 51 [Uppsala: Almqvist & Wiksell, 1989]) settles the discussion by including both versions. This translation is based on the 1905 version of the poem. Because the differences mostly have to do with minor reworkings of stresses and syllables, the translation is fairly true to the first version as well. The 1902 version contains five lines excised in the 1905 version, which I include here: see "The City Journey," note 9.

1. The steam ferry traveled between Stockholm and all the settlements along Lake Mälar west of Stockholm.

2. On Midsummer's Eve, everything is decorated with flowers and leaves, especially birch-leaves.

3. This part of Stockholm forms the shoreline along Lake Mälar.

4. Upswedish men are from central or northern Sweden.

5. Sten Sture the Elder (1440?–1503) was a nephew of King Karl VIII. Sture was regent of Sweden 1470–1503; he assisted in founding the University of Uppsala in 1477 and encouraged the first printing of books in 1483. His son Svante Sture was regent 1503–1512; Sten Sture the Younger, the grandson of Sten Sture the Elder, was regent 1512–1520. Axel Oxenstjerna (1583–1654) was chancellor to Gustav II Adolf and regent

when Gustav Adolf participated in the Thirty Years War and, after his death, while Queen Kristina was still a child. His brother Bengt was a diplomat in the service of Gustav Adolf. Johan Gabriel Oxenstierna (1750–1818) was a court poet to Gustav III and Karl XIII. Gustav Vasa was the first king (1523–1560) of a unified Sweden; under his rule, and largely thanks to Olaus Petri, Sweden converted to Protestantism. Per Brahe (1602–1680), a Swedish soldier and statesman, served under Gustav Adolf. He was governor general of Finland, then a member of the regency after Gustav Adolf's death. Johan Banér (1596–1641) was a general in the Thirty Years War.

6. With Ekollen ("Ekoln"), all the places listed are royal country homes along the banks of Lake Mälar. Most are gone today.

7. The World-Tree, Yggdrasil, in Norse mythology, is an evergreen ash that overshadows the whole world. Its roots and branches bind together heaven and hell. Yggdrasil has three main roots, one in Niflheim (see "The City Journey," note 8), one in Midgard (middle earth), and one in Asgard (the home of the gods). It was a custom in medieval cathedrals to create sculptures of trolls, dragons, and other beasts trapped and trampled at the base of the pillars underneath the nave.

8. This dragon in Norse mythology lives by the eternal spring Hvergelmir in Niflheim, the region of eternal cold and darkness ruled by the goddess Hel.

9. At this point in the text, in the 1905 version of "The City Journey," Strindberg cut five lines from the 1902 version. Translated, they read:

> Dreams not mankind of a golden age as promised by legend?
> Dreams of an innocent peace where lambs may play with the lions?
> Honor to him who desires the good, who yearns to escape from
> Life's degradation and shame and to reach a better existence,
> Woe be the fate of the man who hates what love has united — —

10. In Norse mythology, Ragnarök is the end of the world. See "Loki's Curses," note 2.

"Holy Trinity Night"

The original verse drama fragment, entitled "Valborgsafton på Fagervik" ("Walpurgis Night in Fagervik"), consists mainly of a conversation between the Poet and the Stranger, both social misfits damaged by unhappy love affairs. At the end of the fragment, they decide to travel to Skamsund (Foul Strand) rather than stay in Fagervik (Fair Haven), where people are too happy. These places are important in *A Dream Play* as well. The main section has been transferred almost in its entirety to "Holy Trinity Night" as "Chrysaëtos" (originally sung by the Stranger) and "I Dreamed" (originally sung by the Poet).

1. Fagervik (Fair Haven) is likely modeled on the town Furusund on the east coast of Sweden and north of Stockholm, where Strindberg spent some time visiting rela-

tives soon after returning to Sweden in 1899; he frequently returned there and drew great inspiration from his visits. See Ollén, 169–71.

2. Translated literally, the phrase is: "let the stove grow cold in the shame corner," in other words, let the stove stand in shame and disuse and let us celebrate the return of the warm weather.

3. A *sexa* is a light supper, but *sexa* also means "six." Strindberg makes a gentle pun: a light supper for seven, a six for seven.

4. Filbunk is soured milk with a jellied layer of cream on top.

5. During the week of July 19–24, every name-day is a woman's name. Name-days are celebrated almost like birthdays; especially in Strindberg's time, everyone was named after one of the saints in the church calendar.

6. A Gustavian bed is the Swedish variant of a Louis XVI, an empire style.

7. My translation follows the original *("manglar och ranglar")* here, using nonce words to describe the thunder.

8. By Erik's Day, May 18, the grain is sprouting; by Olof's Day, July 29, the grain is ready for harvest.

9. By Larsmass, August 10, the fruit is ripening.

10. A Swedish variety of apple, it is usually considered to be of the highest quality.

11. Chrysaëtos is not a person but Strindberg's name for the love between Harriet Bosse and himself. In a letter to Harriet from July 1902, during a separation, Strindberg writes: "Is your mission in my life now over? Can there be an end to that which we thought had no beginning? Is Chrysaëtos dead, when the souls are immortal?" (*Letters* 14, 197). The references to a golden eagle ("Gold-Erne") allude to an eagle quill Harriet gave Strindberg with which he used to write. The poet's song "Chrysaëtos" is a rendition of Strindberg's emotional state in September 1901, when Harriet Bosse left him for six weeks. As Ollén observes, the tormented nature and extreme intimacy of the poem make many references obscure or incomprehensible (Ollén, 191). For a detailed account of Strindberg's emotional state at the time he wrote this poem, and for identification of the places he mentions in the poem, see Sven Rinman, "Strindbergs Guldörn," *Svenska diktanalyser,* ed. Magnus von Platen (Stockholm: Bokförlaget Prisma / FIBs Lyrikklubb: Stockholm, 1965), 79–91.

12. The men are creating a road across the frozen lake.

13. Strindberg uses Carl von Linné's term Nemesis Divina here, an arbitrary power against which we are helpless. Strindberg suggests that the love between the two, or possibly the power of the woman's beauty, protects her against this force.

14. According to Ollén, this stanza is deliberately mystifying, a secret message to Harriet that only she would understand (202). He speculates it may have something to do with the conception of their daughter Anne-Marie.

15. That is, the road that runs across the lake is about to be ruined by the icebreaker cutting straight across it.

16. Georg Stiernhjielm (1598–1672), a Swedish poet and scholar, is known as "The Father of Swedish Poetry."

17. This term means the (secret) significance of things. The concept is based on Strindberg's Swedenborgian theories of correspondence and his Linnean natural mysticism.

18. My translation uses a nonce word here, as does the Swedish *(gväar)*.

19. Since "The Vane Sings" contains rhyme that adds significantly to the music of the verse and the sound is here at least as important as the sense, I reproduce the original here, so that the English-speaking reader can at least see how the patterns develop and get an idea of how onomatopoeic the sounds are:

Flöjeln sjunger.

Det sitter en flöjel på ladans tak,
Tobaksladans— — —
Han sjunger bara rakt på sak
Vid nordlig vind— — —

I frost,
Med rost-
igt gap;
Skrap;
Skrap;
Det är en drake
På en hake;
Vassa tänder;
Vinden vänder.
Vip;
Rip;
Lip;
Lipa.
Stripa,
Bladen.
Va sa' den?
Tobaksbladen.

Ala;
Mala;
Snus,
Kardus;
Karduser
Förtjuser

Magistern.
Gardister;
Sprit,
Split
Plit
På baln!
Korpraln!!!

Mästarn,
Tobaksmästarn
På lur
ur, ur, ur,
Ursinning,
Finnig;
irr irr irr
Klirr;
Klirrsporre;
Orre,
Rus,
Sinkadus,
Kris — — —
Polis!!!

*

Det sitter en flöjel på ladans tak,
Tobaksladans
Han visar stundom mera smak,
Vid sydlig vind.
Höst,
Tröst!
Trösta mej!
Brösta dej
Ej!
Järn brytes,
Ljus snytes.
Du hoppas —
Du snoppas.
Draken
På haken
Visslar

Gnisslar
Tänder;
Bänder . .
Vricka —
Err err err,
Spärr —
Spärras?
Förvärras
Slit, slit, slit.
Än en bit.
Vänster Höger
Sorg och Döder
Lip,
Lip.

20. *Snoppa* means not only "to snub" but also "to betray" and "to castrate."
21. Skåne is the southernmost province of Sweden, near Denmark, and is sometimes called Scania in English.

"The Dutchman"

1. Strindberg called both his second wife (Frida Uhl) and his third wife (Harriet Bosse) Omphale, a Lydian queen who owned Hercules as a slave for a time and made him perform many womanly tasks, such as weaving, while she dressed like a man. The myth has deep significance for Strindberg: it fits perfectly his own theories of the battle of brains, the usurping female, and his fears of his own feminine qualities.

"The Wolves Are Howling"

The fire described in the poem probably refers to the famous fire on Sunday, December 30, 1900, and perhaps also to the beacons lighting up Skansen on New Year's Eve, 1899 (Ollén, 303). Skansen, on Djurgården in Stockholm, is an open-air museum started by Arthur Hazelius in 1891 as a way to preserve Swedish folk culture before it disappeared. Buildings from the fifteenth to the nineteenth centuries, from all social strata and from all regions, were collected at Skansen to form a miniature model of Sweden. The animals were added as an afterthought; the decision met with a great deal of controversy, for reasons Strindberg suggests in the poem.

Lotta M. Löfgren is a lecturer in the English department at the University of Virginia, where she teaches drama and twentieth-century literature. She has published articles on African American literature and is currently at work on a full-length book on the plays of Adrienne Kennedy, Suzan-Lori Parks, and Anna Deavere Smith.